NO NONSENSE

FLY FISHING GUIDEBOOKS

Dave Stanley

Fly Fishing Nevada

A Quick, Clear Understanding of
Where to Fly Fish in Nevada
and the Northeastern Sierra

No Nonsense

FLY FISHING GUIDEBOOKS

Author
Dave Stanley

Maps, Illustrations & Production
Pete Chadwell, *Dynamic Arts*
Gary D. Smith, *Performance Design*

Front Cover Photo
Robert Anderson

Back Cover Photo
Robert Anderson

Editors
Jim Yuskavitch & David Banks

Published By
No Nonsense Fly Fishing Guidebooks
P.O. Box 91858
Tucson AZ 85752-1858
www.nononsenseguides.com

Printed in USA

Disclaimer
While this guide will greatly help readers to fly fish, it is not a substitute for caution, good judgment and the services of a qualified fly fishing guide or outfitter.

No Nonsense Fly Fishing Guidebooks believes that in addition to local information and gear, fly fishers need clean water and healthy fish. The publisher encourages preservation, improvement, conservation, enjoyment and understanding of our waters and their inhabitants. A good way to do this is to support organizations dedicated to these ideas.

Acknowledgments

I'm lucky to have so many fine people to thank for their help with this guidebook. Let's start with literally hundreds of Reno Fly Shop customers, friends, and expert anglers who've contributed (in many ways) to what I know about fly fishing in the northeastern Sierra Nevada mountains and in the state of Nevada. Here are the main contributors to my knowledge:

Hugh Chatham Jr. gave me my first fly tying vise. Tiers like Terry Barron and Cal Bird continued to teach and inspire me to use it. Jim and Betty Jackson sold me the fly shop and, with the help of my wife, Janet Stanley, Bud Johnson, and Dave Bryeans, the shop slowly grew through the early difficult years.

Nolan Wells, Sash Nakamoto, Andy Burk, and Cal Cearley are among the best fly fishermen I know. For many years they've unselfishly shared their observations, techniques, flies, and favorite waters with me.

My talented partner Jeff Cavender shares my enthusiasm for all aspects of fly fishing. His wisdom and wit make working with him a joy. In fact, this book would not have been possible without Jeff's prodding, editing, rewriting, and information gathering.

Finally, thanks to everyone who loves, respects and preserves the natural beauty of the areas covered in this guide and the other special places like them.

—Dave Stanley

Dedication

This guidebook is dedicated to my family.

Helen and Dave Stanley Sr. gave me my first fly rod when I was six years old. They always made sure there was time for fishing adventures on waters near and far.

My wife, Janet, shares my dreams, supports me always, and is a wonderful mother to our children, John David and Katie.

They continually make fly fishing, and life, new and exciting.
—*Dave Stanley*

Fly Fishing in Nevada & the Northeastern Sierra

Some thoughts on the state, conservation, and the future

Nevada is our nation's sixth largest state, and approximately 90 percent of this land is public. The diverse geography includes many mountain ranges with peaks higher than 10,000 feet, huge expanses of alkali and near-barren desert, aspen-filled canyons, and oceans of sagebrush that reach beyond the horizon.

In a state with such an abundance of natural wealth, there is one commodity in relatively short supply—water. Fortunately for fly fishermen, in most places where water exists, so do fisheries.

There are many demands on Nevada's water resources: mining, cattle ranching, farming, casino gambling, and ever-expanding development. All have negatively affected many fisheries in the last century. The good news is that a growing number of these industries, with guidance from the Nevada Department of Wildlife, have become aware of the economic as well as aesthetic value of fisheries in a state known for its desert landscape.

The Pyramid Lake Paiute Tribe for example, has spent millions of dollars and thousands of hours in court battling to keep adequate fresh water flowing down the Truckee River. This will ensure that Pyramid Lake's populations of endangered cui-cui chub and world-record Lahontan cutthroat will have an environment in which to propagate. Efforts such as these are commendable and necessary for the future of fishing in Nevada.

One of the great challenges in writing this guide is not spoiling what is out there. Rest assured that, in Nevada and the Sierra there are scores of pristine, free-flowing mountain streams and small- to medium-sized lakes and reservoirs where the quality of the experience isn't necessarily measured in inches or pounds. Most of these places will not be identified in the pages that follow. Pay your dues, do your research, and give generously to the next fly fishing guide you encounter and you may find out about some of these secret spots.

The waters we discuss in this guidebook are those that are easily reached by most anglers and are generally well known.

If you are an avid backpacker or horseback rider and want to avoid crowds, the "wilderness experience" is available in Nevada and the northeastern Sierra. The Desolation Wilderness, Great Basin National Park, and remote mountain ranges such as Toiyabe, Moniter, Ruby, and Jarbidge all provide solitude. Outfitters are available to get you into these places if you don't want to do it yourself. Should you decide to explore these areas, keep in mind that many of the waters there are small and fragile. Leave them in better shape than you found them. We hope that the angler who came before or will come after you will do the same.

Drought is an annual possibility in much of Nevada, and the waters we discuss in this guide are subject to low water conditions. Anglers planning to visit our state should contact one or more of the local sources listed in the back of this book for up-to-date information before planning a trip. While low water often provides excellent fishing, sometimes it ruins it. It's best to know well in advance what you might be getting into.

In Nevada, casino gaming, skiing, and a wide variety of outdoor activities provide the visiting angler with many other leisure opportunities. An often-overlooked bonus to fishing in Nevada is that many of our lakes and streams don't close. Wintertime fishing is both challenging and generally uncrowded.

In the many years we have been in the fly fishing industry, it never ceases to amaze us how many people discount the fishing opportunities in the Silver State. Most view crossing Nevada as a necessary evil to reach the better known, as well as more crowded, waters of Idaho, Wyoming, Montana, and California. This is not the worst thing in the world, but many anglers are missing out on outdoor experiences that almost always rate a 10, even if the fishing doesn't. Give Nevada a try…you won't be disappointed!

Contents

Acknowledgments.. 5

Dedication 7

Fly Fishing in Nevada & the Northeastern Sierra................. 8

Nevada Vicinity Map 10

Fly Fishing Conditions by the Month 11

The Nevada No Nonsense Fly-O-Matic................................ 12

Common Game Fish in Nevada & the Northeastern Sierra..... 16

The Best Flies to Use in Nevada & the Northeastern Sierra 17

Top Nevada & the Northeastern Sierra Fly Fishing Waters

Carson River, East Fork.. 21

Crittenden Reservoir.. 23

Denio Junction Area 25

Eagle Lake 27

Frenchman Lake 29

Hobart Creek Reservoir 31

Illipah Reservoir, Comins Lake, & Cave Lake 33

Jackson Meadows & Milton Reservoirs.............................. 35

Lake Davis 37

Martis Creek Lake 39

Mason Valley Wildlife Management Area 41

Pyramid Lake 43

Ruby Lake 45

Sheep Creek Reservoir 47

South Fork Reservoir 49

Spooner Lake 51

Stampede, Boca, & Prosser Creek Reservoirs 53

Truckee River, CA... 55

Truckee River, NV 57

Walker River, East Fork... 59

Wild Horse & Wilson Reservoirs.. 61

Other Nevada Rivers, Streams & Creeks............................. 63

Other Nevada Still Waters 65

Appendix

Nevada Fly Fishing Resources 66

Where No Nonsense Guides Come From............................ 69

No Nonsense Fly Fishing Knots 70

Find Your Way with No Nonsense Guides........................... 72

Notes.. 78

Nevada Highway Network 80

Nevada Vicinity Map

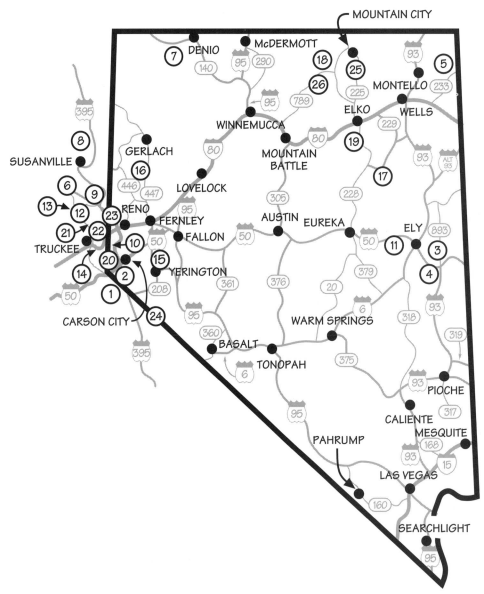

Referenced Streams, Lakes, and Reservoirs

1. Carson River, East Fork, CA
2. Carson River, East Fork, NV
3. Cave Lake
4. Comins lake
5. Crittenden Reservoir
6. Davis Lake
7. Denio Junction Area
8. Eagle Lake
9. Frenchman Lake
10. Hobart Creek Reservoir
11. Illipah Reservoir
12. Jackson Meadows Reservoir
13. Milton Reservoir
14. Martis Creek Reservoir
15. Mason Valley Wildlife Management Area
16. Pyramid Lake
17. Ruby Lake
18. Sheep Creek Reservoir
19. South Fork Reservoir
20. Spooner Lake
21. Stampede, Boca, & Prosser Creek Reservoirs
22. Truckee River, CA
23. Truckee River, NV
24. Walker River, East Fork
25. Wild Horse Reservoir
26 Wilson Sink Reservoir

Conditions by the Month
Nevada Fly Fishing

Legend — FEATURED WATERS:
(1) REFERS TO NUMBERS ON VICINITY MAP · ■ BEST · ▨ GOOD · ▢ FAIR · N NO FISHING

#	FEATURED WATERS	JAN	FEB	MAR	APR	MAY	JUN	JUL	AUG	SEP	OCT	NOV	DEC
1	Carson River, East Fork, CA	N	N	N	N							N	N
2	Carson River, East Fork, NV												
3	Cave Lake												
4	Comins lake												
5	Crittenden Reservoir												
6	Davis Lake	N	N										N
7	Denio Junction Area	N	N	N	N							N	N
8	Eagle Lake	N	N	N	N	N							
9	Frenchman Lake	N	N										N
10	Hobart Creek Reservoir	N	N	N	N						N	N	N
12 13	Jackson Meadows & Milton Reservoirs	N	N	N	N							N	N
14	Martis Creek Reservoir	N	N	N	N							N	N
15	Mason Valley Wildlife Management Area	N									N	N	N
16	Pyramid Lake							N	N	N			
17	Ruby Lake												
18	Sheep Creek Reservoir												
19	South Fork Reservoir												
20	Spooner Lake	N	N	N								N	N
21	Stampede, Boca, & Prosser Creek Reservoirs	N	N	N									N
22	Truckee River, CA	N	N	N								N	N
23	Truckee River, NV												
24	Walker River, East Fork, CA	N	N	N								N	N
24	Walker River, East Fork, NV												
25	Wild Horse Reservoir	N	N									N	N
26	Wilson Sink Reservoir	N	N									N	N

The Nevada No Nonsense Fly-O-Matic
A Quick-Start Guide for Fly Fishing Nevada & Northeastern Sierra

Game Fish

Rainbow, brown, cutthroat, tiger, and brook trout are found throughout our area. Other coldwater species include kokanee salmon and lake trout. Warmwater species available to the fly fisherman include largemouth bass, smallmouth bass, striped bass, white bass, wipers (striped bass and white bass hybrid), walleyed pike, northern pike, crappie, and a variety of sunfish.

Catch and Release

Some Nevada waters have no-kill or limited-kill regulations, but most do not. Responsible anglers should try to return their fish to fight another day. Be careful handling fish too; use a net or release tool when possible and return fish to the water immediately. In August and September surface temperatures of many lakes and reservoirs are higher than trout like. In these conditions, don't overplay hooked fish; release them quickly.

Weather

In the Sierra and many of the high desert ranges, weather changes can be fast and drastic. The old saying "If you don't like the weather, just wait 10 minutes" applies here. It can snow at altitude in any month of the year. In fall, winter, and spring be prepared for extreme weather. Cloudbursts in the summer months often muddy up the water briefly and can make driving on unimproved roads very hazardous.

Hazards and Safety

Common sense will help you more than anything here. A few things you might want to consider:

Use a wading staff in fast, rocky streams and on narrow, rocky trails. In rocky areas, be careful where you step. Falls and rattlesnakes can ruin a fishing trip.

Float tubers are required to have a Coast Guard-approved flotation device either worn or attached to their tube.

Be aware of hypothermia and its effects on you. Float tubers are particularly susceptible to this, as are anglers without adequate rain gear and warm clothes.

Don't drink untreated water unless it is from a springhead. Some of it is OK, but *Giardia* is common.

Altitude sickness, sunburn, and dehydration affect many anglers every year. Take appropriate measures to avoid these problems.

Violent lightning storms can appear quickly on summer afternoons. Get off the water and put down your fly rod.

Warm summer temperatures dry out the range and forests and create dangerous fire conditions. Please use every precaution when traveling, camping, and fishing here. Drive unimproved roads that you are not familiar with only in the daytime. At night use caution on highways as wild horses, range cattle, deer, and other wildlife inhabit many of these areas and wander on to the asphalt.

Always tell someone where you are going and when you expect to return.

Desert Reservoirs

Many of the small- to medium-sized impoundments in the wilds of Nevada are at least partially spring fed. These nutrient-rich environments support large populations of midges, scuds, snails, damsels, and leeches. Fly fishers should come prepared with a selection of these patterns. When things get tough, there are few still waters in Nevada where a size #8–14 Woolly Bugger in olive, brown, or black won't catch fish. For those anglers hunting large trout, these waters produce large numbers of them.

Small Streams

Trout in these waters are not particularly selective. Standard dries such as Adams, Humpies, Wulffs, and Elk Hair Caddis will serve you well in sizes #12–18. Nymphs such as the Prince, Bird's Nest, Zug Bug, and Hare's Ear will also bring strikes from hungry trout. Add a few terrestrials (Ants, Beetles, Hoppers) and a Muddler Minnow or Woolly Bugger and your fly selection is complete. Shorter fly rods (7 feet) will serve you better on many of these waters. Streamside vegetation and small target areas require accurate casts. Fish upstream where possible and sneak up on the fish, as they tend to be easily spooked in these small environs.

Rivers

If you want to catch fish regularly on Nevada-area rivers, concentrate on nymph fishing. A good selection of nymphs, strike indicators, and split shot are all you need. It can be said that the difference between a good nymph angler and a great nymph angler is one split shot! This is true. If your fly is on or near the bottom you will catch more fish. Casting upstream and fishing your indicator in the same drag-free manner you would a dry fly is the most popular technique. Some anglers prefer to use a dry fly as their indicator, this works well in some situations. Don't try to cover a lot of water when nymph fishing. Be persistent and fish good holding water thoroughly.

Streamer fishing is often overlooked by many fly fishers. Most of our rivers hold large populations of baitfish and sculpins. Muddler Minnows, Zonkers, Woolly Buggers, and other similar imitations work well when fished on floating or sinking lines. The patient angler in Nevada has the opportunity to

land some large fish with these flies.

Dry fly fishing can be good through the summer and early fall. The best hatch activity usually involves caddis and little yellow stones on summer evenings. Mayfly hatches provide good morning and some evening activity throughout the season. Terrestrials, when present, can also produce good action. Consult local information sources in the back of this book (especially if you are a dry fly enthusiast) because conditions can change quickly.

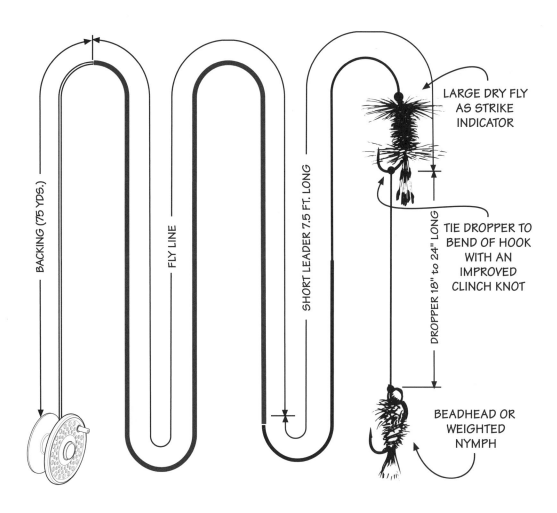

Using a large dry fly as a strike indicator can be very effective in Nevada, Use the dry fly as you would a strike indicator, except that this "strike indicator" will hook a fish that rolls on it! Tie the dropper directly to the bend of the hook using an improved clinch knot.

Rods
If we had to pick one all-around rod to fish these waters, a 9 foot 5 weight is a great choice. For small, brushy streams a shorter (7 foot) 3–5 weight rod is an advantage. For float tubers, a long 9½–10 foot rod is often better. Warmwater species such as stripers, wipers, and largemouth require bigger tackle (6–8 weight) because of the size of the flies and sometimes the fish. More often than not, wind is a factor, so choose tackle accordingly.

Reels
Single-action fly reels with click or disk drags are adequate for most of these waters, but they should hold at least 75–100 yards of backing, particularly if you fish lakes and reservoirs for large trout.

Lines and Leaders
Most stream and river fishing can be done with a floating line. Occasionally a sink tip or sinking line is an advantage when fishing streamers. For lakes

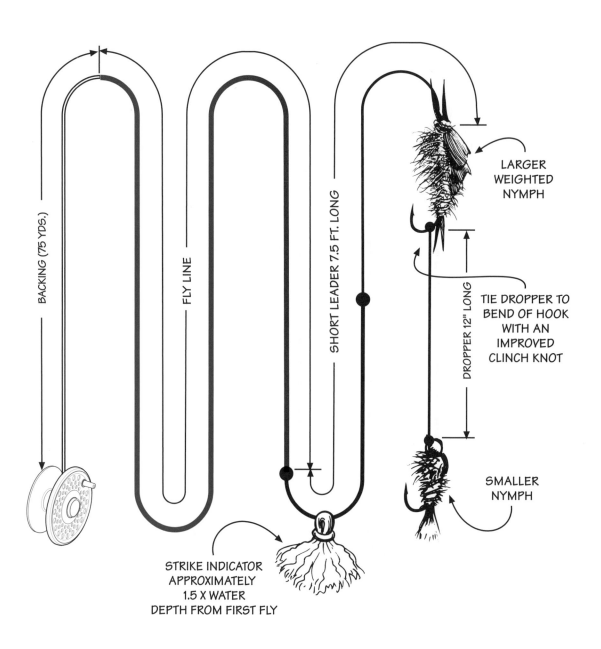

Another popular two-fly rig for fly fishing in Nevada uses a typical strike indicator placed on the butt section of the leader roughly 1-½ times the water depth from the first fly. Use a large weighted nymph as the first fly, and then add a dropper and use a smaller nymph as a "trailer."

and reservoirs, packing a full complement of lines will improve your success. These include floating, intermediate/slow sinking, a type two fast sinking, and an extra-fast sinking (preferably a shooting head) for Pyramid Lake. In late summer and other warmwater situations, when trout are holding in deeper water, these fast-sinking lines are the ticket.

Leaders should generally be short and stout for sinking lines (6–7½ foot 2X–4X). For dry fly fishing and floating line nymphing, 9–10 foot leaders in 4X–6X cover most situations.

Wading Gear

Felt-soled shoes are a must in our rivers. A wading staff or cleats is also advisable. Wet-wading is usually comfortable during the summer months. Float tubers should come prepared with neoprene chest waders and adequate warm clothing, as should stream fishermen in the fall, winter, and spring.

Guides

Nevada and California require fishing guides to be licensed. Hiring a guide for a day or two during your stay will shorten your learning curve considerably. When booking a trip, make sure you let the guide know the type of fishing you want to do. Be realistic about your physical abilities and fishing capabilities. This makes for a much more enjoyable day on the water.

Private Fly Fishing Waters

Many fly fishers, particularly those in the beginning and intermediate learning stages, can benefit greatly from time spent at a "pay-to-play" fishery. The opportunity to hook, fight, land, and release good numbers of medium to large trout provides an education that can take years on more difficult public waters. The three operations listed here offer excellent still water fishing (weather permitting) in remote and scenic locations. They are good value and can be booked through most area fly shops.

Goodrich Creek
15 miles from Susanville, California

Winnemucca Ranch
25 miles north of Reno, Nevada

Smith Creek Ranch
20 miles southwest of Austin, Nevada

Contact information for guiding:
Reno Fly Shop, (775) 825-3474,
www.renoflyshop.com

Crowding Considerations

Many of our waters are off the beaten path, so crowding is not typically a problem. When you do encounter other anglers, give them plenty of room (especially if they were there first)! On more popular waters be prepared for crowds during holidays and when the fishing is awesome. Always treat the fishery and the surrounding environment with care and leave it cleaner than you found it.

Licensing

Because of the rural nature dominating much of Northern Nevada, you should buy a license when you pass through a major town or city. Many small towns do not have a license agent.

2005 Fishing Licenses

Annual Resident License $29.00
Annual Non-Resident License $69.00
Resident Short Term License
$9.00 for the first day
$3.00 for each consecutive day after
Non-Resident Short Term License
$18.00 for the first day
$7.00 for each consecutive day after
Trout Stamp
(required in waters with trout) $10.00

Note: Nevada annual licenses are currently valid from March 1st through the end of the following February.

Ratings

It is difficult to assign a rating number to a fishery that anglers interpret differently. The ratings in this guide combine our views of the available fishing, ease or difficulty of access, and the natural surroundings. Occasionally extra-credit points were given for monster hatches, monster fish, great sunsets, and such other phenomena. All of the waters discussed here provide *good* fly fishing experiences. You just have to fish them all to determine which you think are the best.

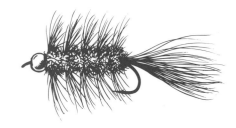

Common Game Fish in Nevada & Northeastern Sierra

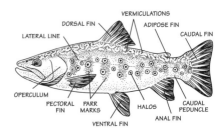

Typical salmon, trout, or char.
Most hatchery fish have a clipped adipose fin.

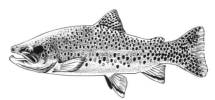

BROWN TROUT

Brown-colored back with big black spots.
A square tail and black and red spots on sides
with light blue rings. Hard to catch,
easily spooked.

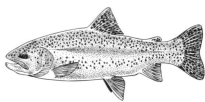

RAINBOW TROUT

The most abundant wild and hatchery fish. An
olive-bluish back with small black spots. Sides
have light red or pink band. Lake 'bows are
often all silver.

BROOK TROUT

Actually char (Dolly Varden, bull trout, lake
trout, etc.). Black, blue-gray, or green back;
mottled light-colored markings. Sides have
red spots with blue rings. Square tail. Lower
fins red, striped with black and white.
Prefers cold water.

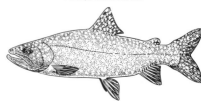

LAKE TROUT

In the char family. Back color is light gray
or green. White spots cover back and sides.
Indented or split tail.

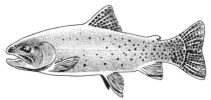

LAHONTAN CUTTHROAT TROUT

Red or orange marks under jaws. Brownish
green colored back, large black spots on tail
decreasing in number towards head. Red-
range or rose colored on sides and pink or
yellow underneath.

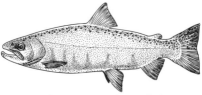

KOKANEE SALMON

Green-blue back with speckles. Sides and
belly silver. Fall spawning turns color to dark
red, leathery skin with green head. Male snout
hooks and back humps, female body shape
stays like trout.

STRIPED BASS

Greenish back, 7–8 horizontal stripes on silver
background on sides. Spiny dorsal fin attached
to soft dorsal fin. Longer than other bass.

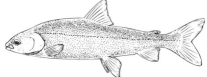

MOUNTAIN WHITEFISH

Light brown to whitish, split tail. Mouth
smaller than trout and doesn't extend back
past the eye.

CRAPPIE, BLUEGILL

Crappie, bluegill, and other sunfish: silver,
bluish, or greenish with dark green or black
splotches on the sides. Compressed body.
Spines on dorsal, anal fins.

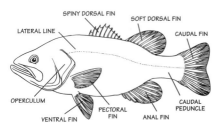

Typical bass, perch, crappie.

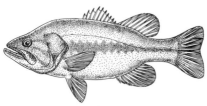

LARGEMOUTH BASS

Dark green back and sides with dark band of
irregular spots along sides. Spiny dorsal fin
(9–10 rays) separated from soft dorsal fin by
deep notch. Closed upper jaw extends to rear
or beyond rear of eyes.

SMALLMOUTH BASS

Dark brown back with vertical bronze stripes
on the sides. Spiny dorsal fin (9–10 spines) has
no deep notch separating the soft
dorsal fin.

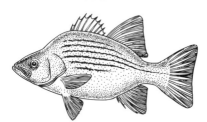

WHITE BASS

Similar to a striped bass, more silvery. Stripes
less pronounced.

WIPER BASS

Wiper, hybrid of white and striped bass.
Horizontal lines are broken.

 Illustrations by Pete Chadwell. For fine art and fish renderings, contact: Dynamic Arts, 61858 Avonlea Circle, Bend, Oregon 97702. www.dynamicarts.com

The Best Flies to Use in Nevada & Northeastern Sierra

TROUT

ELK HAIR CADDIS

BLUE-WINGED OLIVE

PARACHUTE ADAMS

ROYAL WULFF

COMPARADUN

BURK'S
ADULT DAMSEL

ADAMS

HUMPY

CUTTER'S MIDGE
EMERGER

MARTIS MIDGE

MINI BEADHEAD
SHEEP CREEK

SNAIL

ZUG BUG

PRINCE

SCUD

BIRD'S NEST

BOB'S
MARABOU DAMSEL

HARE'S EAR NYMPH

GIANT MIDGE

PHEASANT TAIL
SOFT HACKLE

ZONKER

SHEEP CREEK SPECIAL

MUDDLER MINNOW

STAYNOR DUCKTAIL

BEADHEAD WOOLLY BUGGER

MARABOU LEECH

MATUKA

BASS

WHITLOCK'S DEER HAIR POPPER

BLANTON'S WHISTLER

CLOUSER MINNOW DEEP

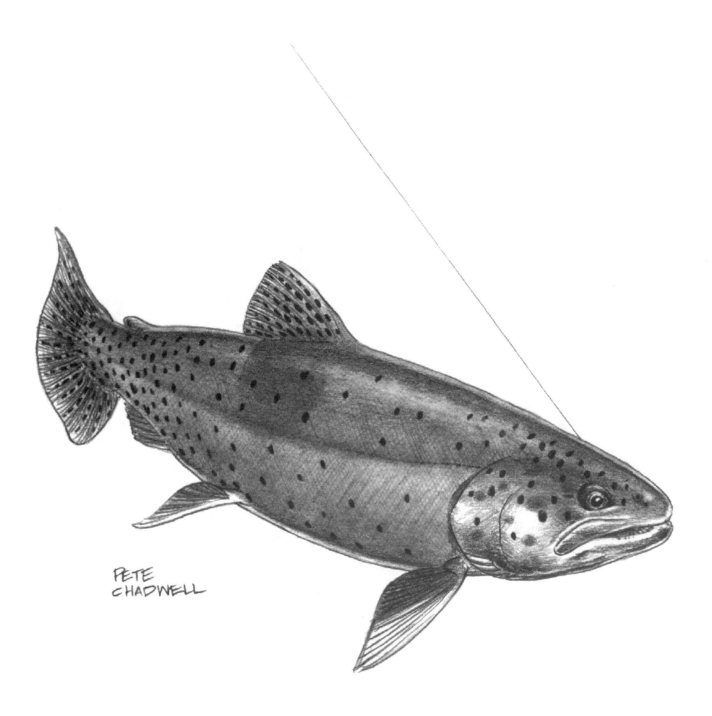

Lahontan Cutthroat Trout

Top Nevada & Northeastern Sierra Fly Fishing Waters

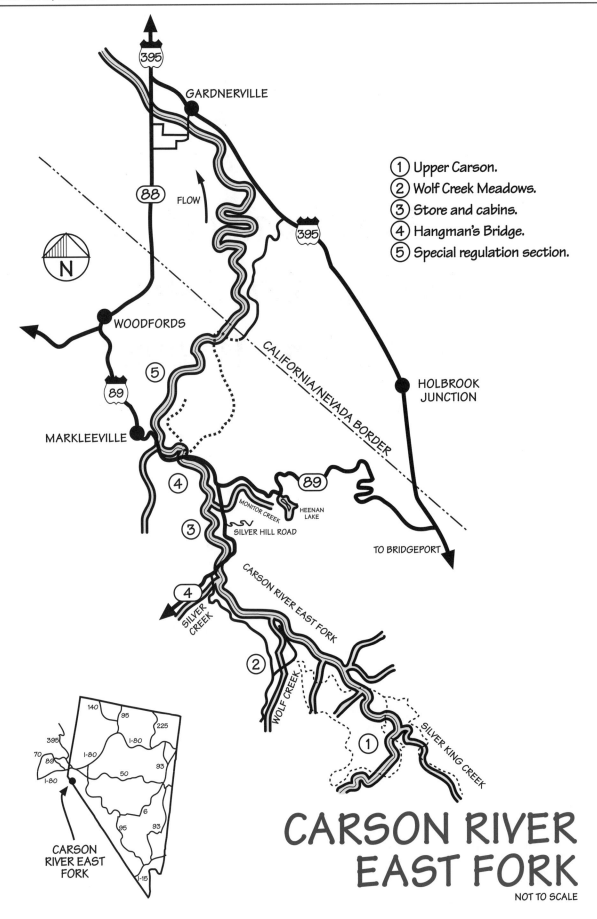

① Upper Carson.
② Wolf Creek Meadows.
③ Store and cabins.
④ Hangman's Bridge.
⑤ Special regulation section.

CARSON RIVER
EAST FORK
NOT TO SCALE

Carson River
East Fork

If solitude in mountain splendor is what you like, the East Fork of the Carson is perfect. This stream provides trout anglers with many different experiences (access being one). The narrow, fast-flowing upper reaches, above Wolf Creek, are accessible only by a rough 4WD trail, on horseback, or by foot. This is a classic freestone stream with lots of riffles, rapids, deep runs, and pools. These conditions create excellent habitat for stoneflies, caddisflies, and some species of mayflies throughout the Carson drainage.

As is typical on this type of water, nymph and wet fly fishing methods produce fish throughout the season. Usually late in the evening, during the warmer months of summer, there is excellent dry fly fishing. The large numbers of baitfish also mean success is likely for skilled streamer anglers.

The river from Wolf Creek down to Hangman's Bridge (just outside of Markleeville, California) has several inflow tributaries that make the river grow dramatically. Here, less adventuresome anglers have relatively easy access off Highway 89 and Highway 4.

From Hangman's Bridge to the Nevada state line is a special regulation river section, accessible only by 4WD, on foot or, in good water years, raft or pontoon boat. Large fish are consistently taken in this stretch.

The river remains a viable trout fishery where it enters Nevada and passes through the Gardnerville area. Beyond this point the river changes to primarily a warmwater fishery as it flows toward Lahontan Reservoir, although trout can still be found here and there.

To get to the East Fork of the Carson from the California side, take Highway 50 past Lake Tahoe to Highway 89 south. After about 12 miles take Highway 88 and follow the signs to Markleeville, California. The river parallels the highway.

To get there from Reno, take Highway 395 south to Minden, Nevada. Take Highway 88 west to Woodfords, California, and the junction of Highways 88, 89 and 4.

Type of Fish
Rainbow, cutthroat, and brown trout. Mountain whitefish. Brook trout in tributaries.

Known Hatches
Like the Truckee and Walker rivers, caddis are prolific here. Mayflies appear in March, hatching sporadically through late September and early October. Golden stones hatch March through April prior to or just at the beginning of runoff, and little yellow stones appear in June through August.

Equipment to Use
Rods: 5 or 6 weight, 9'.
Line: Floating, occasionally sink tips for deep water.
Leaders: 7½–10', 3X–6X.
Reels: Standard trout reels are fine.
Wading: Felt-soled boots, chest-high neoprenes.

Flies to Use
Dry patterns: Elk Hair Caddis, Adams, Humpy, Royal Wulff, Parachute Hare's Ear, other parachute patterns in various colors, Little Yellow Stones, Stimulators, Ants, and Hoppers.

Nymphs: Bird's Nest, Gold Ribbed Hare's Ear, Prince, Zug Bug, any of these with beadhead. Green Rockworm, Golden Stone, Little Yellow Stone, Western Coachman, Soft Hackles, Caddis Pupa, and Emergers.
Streamers: Muddler Minnow, Woolly Bugger, Hornberg, Zonker, Matuka.

When to Fish
Depending on runoff, June through July and September through October usually have the best dry fly action. Nymph throughout the season. Streamers work well in the cooler waters of spring and fall.

Seasons & Limits
Nevada: Open all year.
California: Last Saturday in April to November 15. There are special regulations in California. Check the appropriate state regulations!

Accommodations & Services
All services are readily available in larger towns like Gardnerville & Carson City, Nevada, and Markleeville, California.

Rating
Good dry fly, nymph, and streamer fishing; the East Fork of the Carson rates a solid 8.

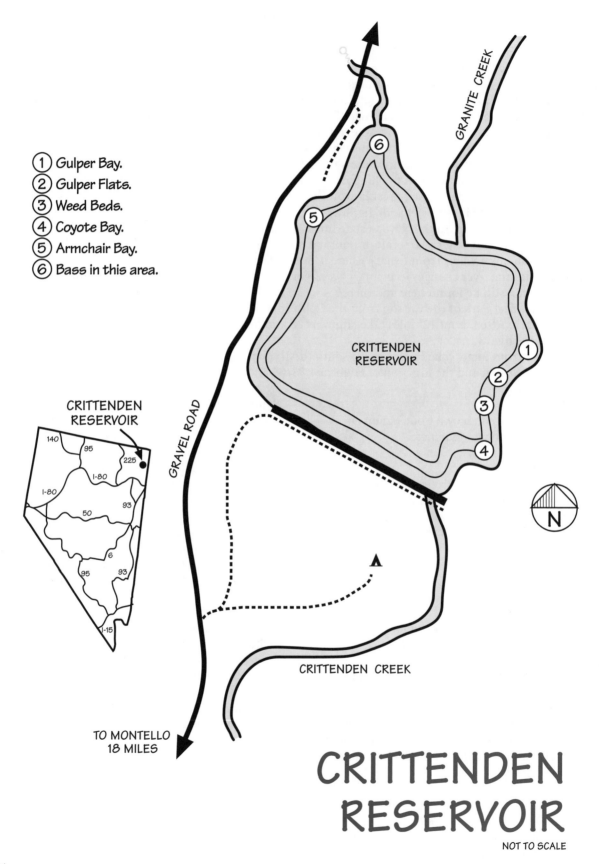

1. Gulper Bay.
2. Gulper Flats.
3. Weed Beds.
4. Coyote Bay.
5. Armchair Bay.
6. Bass in this area.

GRANITE CREEK

6

5

CRITTENDEN
RESERVOIR

1

2

3

4

GRAVEL ROAD

CRITTENDEN
RESERVOIR

140
95
225
I-80
I-80
93
50
6
95
93
I-15

N

CRITTENDEN CREEK

TO MONTELLO
18 MILES

CRITTENDEN RESERVOIR

NOT TO SCALE

Crittenden Reservoir

If you're willing to make a long drive to a remote location, here are the directions to some of the best still water fly fishing in Nevada. Take Interstate 80 to the Montello exit, 25 miles east of Wells, Nevada. Drive northeast on State Highway 233 into Montello, and then bear due north on a gravel road for approximately 18 miles. You'll arrive at a small reservoir of about 70 or so surface acres.

Crittenden possesses clear, relatively shallow water (only 30' deep or so, at the southeast corner by the dam), abundant insect life, and football-shaped trout of which fly fishing dreams are made. Most rainbows run up to 18". A trophy largemouth bass weighs in at five pounds, though smaller bass are more common in Crittenden.

In the spring, despite varying weather conditions, you can have very productive morning and afternoon fishing. Use an intermediate or sink tip line and Gold Ribbed Hare's Ear; Damsel Nymph; or small, dark Leech patterns. If this isn't enough, take out your dry line and one of a variety of Mayfly Emergers or Dun patterns and fish the callibaetis hatch. This hatch seems to arrive like clockwork every day. In June and July switch your midday surface tactics to accommodate the trout and bass that crash on adult Damsel patterns. We're sure you'll not feel shortchanged.

In the fall, hatches tail off, but the fishing doesn't. Twitch small Midge Pupa and Scud patterns, suspended under an indicator and dry line. You'll still get a goodly number of the powerful takes, characteristic of Crittenden's strong, acrobatic trout. This time of year, again try a Gold Ribbed Hare's Ear or Leech pattern, slowly retrieved, on a sinking line. This technique is almost always productive.

Type of Fish
Hybrid rainbows and largemouth bass.

Known Hatches
Damsels, dragonflies, mayflies, caddis, and midges.

Equipment to Use
Rods: 4–6 weight 8½'–9'.
Reels: Click or disk to balance rod.
Lines: Floating, intermediate, and II full-sink. Or II, 10' sink tip to match the rod.
Leaders: Sinking lines, 6'–7½', 3X–5X. Floating lines, 9'–12', 4X–6X.
Wading: A float tube or small (cartop) boat is best.

Flies to Use
Trout
Dry patterns: Gray Humpies, Callibaetis Comparaduns and Cripples, suspended Midge patterns, Adult Damsels.
Nymphs: Soft Hackle and small Pheasant Tail (greased and fished just under the surface), Monster Midge Larva and Pupa patterns, Gold Ribbed Hare's Ears, Damsel and Dragon patterns, Snail, Scud, or small peacock bodies like Zug Bug or Prince.
Streamers: Olive, Brown, or Black Woolly Buggers and Matuka.

Bass
Assorted Poppers and Dahlberg Divers. Black and Brown Bear Hair streamers and Woolly Buggers.

When to Fish
For trout, the best fishing is in the spring and fall. Fish for bass throughout the summer.

Seasons & Limits
Open year-round. Fishing allowed one hour before sunrise to two hours after sunset. Limit one trout over 17" and five bass, none between 10" and 13". Artificial flies and lures only. Boats and motors are permitted, but no water skiing. Verify current regulations for any changes.

Accommodations & Services
No established campgrounds, no lakeside camping. Unimproved camping areas are located close to the lake. The closest services of any sort are in Montello, Nevada.

Rating
In the spring and fall this water deserves at least an 8. On one of those special days it's a 10. During the summer, the bass fishing rates a 7 or 8 while the trout fishing drops to a 5.

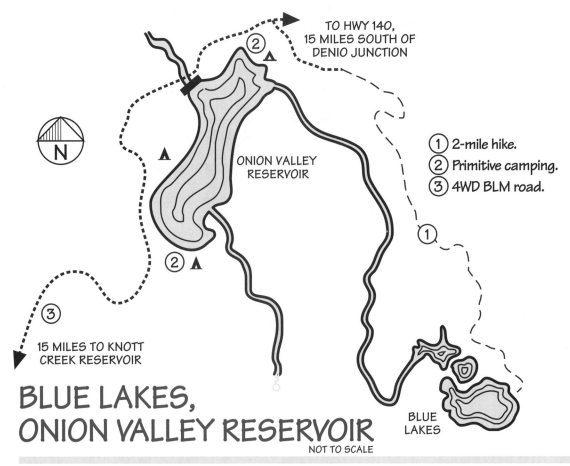

TO HWY 140,
15 MILES SOUTH OF
DENIO JUNCTION

ONION VALLEY
RESERVOIR

N

① 2-mile hike.
② Primitive camping.
③ 4WD BLM road.

15 MILES TO KNOTT
CREEK RESERVOIR

BLUE LAKES,
ONION VALLEY RESERVOIR

BLUE
LAKES

NOT TO SCALE

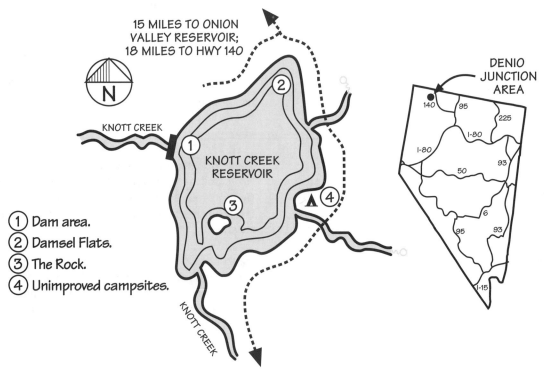

15 MILES TO ONION
VALLEY RESERVOIR;
18 MILES TO HWY 140

N

KNOTT CREEK

KNOTT CREEK
RESERVOIR

① Dam area.
② Damsel Flats.
③ The Rock.
④ Unimproved campsites.

KNOTT CREEK

DENIO
JUNCTION
AREA

140 95   225

I-80

I-80   93

50

6   93

95   93

I-15

KNOTT CREEK RESERVOIR

NOT TO SCALE

Denio Junction Area

For still water fly fishers, the Denio Junction area of northern Nevada ranks just this side of heaven. Four scenic reservoirs, Big Spring, Knott Creek, Onion Valley, and Blue Lakes, are located in this remote, high-desert country. As the crow flies, these impoundments are reasonably close to to one another. The short drive to each water is sometimes hair-raising. While only the road to Knott Creek has a section where 4WD is mandatory, dirt roads in the desert can quickly become vehicle traps after even a brief summer rain shower. Go prepared with a shovel and related equipment! Many use chains and 4WD during spring and fall rains.

The fly fishing is worth it. All of these reservoirs are excellent fisheries, each rating a 9 or above for sizable trout alone. Use a variety of dry fly and nymph patterns. Streamers fished on sinking lines can be productive too, especially for bigger fish.

Big Spring Reservoir (not on map), as you might guess from its name, is fed by a large spring. The Nevada Division of Wildlife dammed it to create this several-hundred-acre impoundment. The spring keeps the water cool most of the year. But when the wind blows, as it does almost every afternoon, this shallow reservoir can turn into chocolate milk. Winters with below-average snowfall also negatively affect this fishery. It is wise to check on current conditions before traveling to Big Spring.

Onion Valley Reservoir and Blue Lakes are close together. You can drive to Onion Valley, then take a short hike to Blue Lakes. If you're into numbers, both still waters provide excellent opportunities to catch many 12" to 16" trout and the occasional whopper.

For trophy fishing, Knott Creek Reservoir is the place to go. Due to special regulations (put in place several years ago), this fishery has been regularly producing trout of five pounds or more. There's also an abundance of 16" to 21" fish. This is as good as still water fishing gets in Nevada.

To get to these waters from Nevada, go to Winnemucca and take Highway 95 north to Highway 140. Take 140 about 50 miles west and north. About 13 miles south of Denio Junction look for a highway maintenance station. Turn left on the gravel road and drive mostly west about 18 miles to the Onion Valley Reservoir or Blue Lakes sign.

Type of Fish

Primarily rainbow trout fisheries. There are a few browns, brookies, and cutbows. Knott Creek has a very healthy population of tiger trout.

Known Hatches

Damsels, callibaetis mayflies, and midges.

Equipment to Use

Rods: 4–6 weight, 8½'–9'.
Reels: Click or disk balanced to rod.
Lines: Floating, intermediate and II sink.
Leaders: Sinking lines, 6'–7½', 3X–5X. For floating 9'–12', 4X–6X.
Wading: All have wading access. Sometimes it's preferable to wade, but a float tube or pram can also be useful. Use neoprene waders and felt-soled boots when the water or weather is cold. Lightweight waders are OK when temperatures warm up.

Flies to Use

Dry patterns: Giant and smaller suspended Midge patterns, Adult Damsels, Callibaetis Paranymphs, Parachute Adams, Parachute Hare's Ear, Mosquito.
Nymphs: Small Soft Hackle, Pheasant Tail, greased and fished just under the surface. Brassie, #10–20 Midge Larva and Pupa. Black and Olive Bird's Nest, Damsel and Dragonfly, Snail, Scud, Small Peacock-body Zug Bug or Prince.
Streamers: Olive, Brown, or Black Woolly Bugger, Leeches, Staynor Ducktail, Sheep Creek Special. Floating Black Foam Zonker for spectacular night fishing.

When to Fish

Best from season opening until mid-July and again from Labor Day until the lakes close.

Seasons & Limits

Big Spring and Onion Valley Reservoirs and Blue Lakes: Open the second Saturday in June through November 15.
Knott Creek: The second Saturday in May to the second Saturday in June is catch and release only. Artificial lures or flies with single barbless hooks only. Always check current regulations.

Accommodations & Services

Limited gas, food, and lodging at Denio Junction. The closest really complete services are 100 miles away in Winnemucca, Nevada, or 70 miles away in Lakeview, Oregon.

Rating

Early in the season until mid-July and from mid-Sept. through October all of these still waters rate 8 or 9.

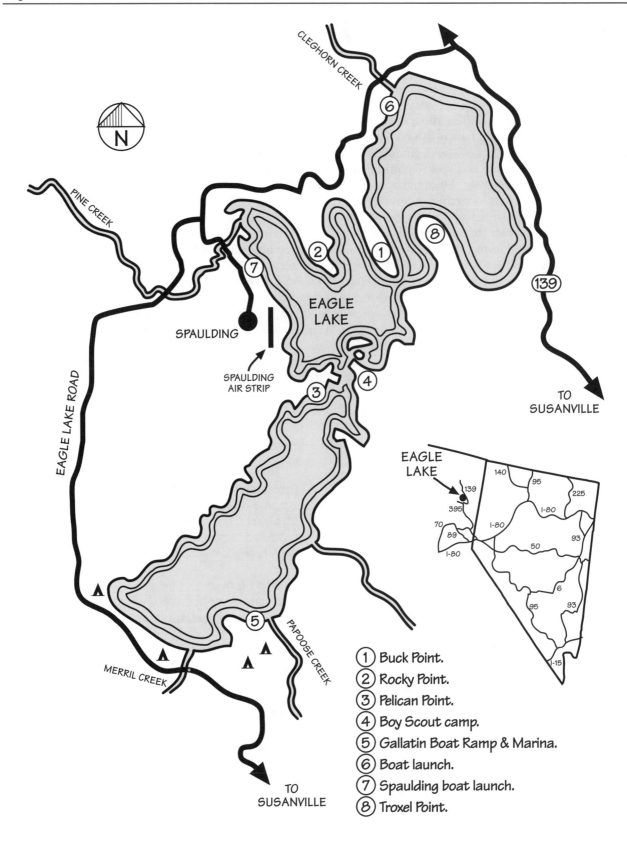

N

CLEGHORN CREEK

PINE CREEK

EAGLE LAKE ROAD

⑥

⑦

② ①

⑧

EAGLE
LAKE

SPAULDING

SPAULDING
AIR STRIP

③

④

139

TO
SUSANVILLE

⑤

PAPOOSE CREEK

MERRIL CREEK

TO
SUSANVILLE

EAGLE
LAKE

140
395
70
89
I-80
I-80
I-80
50
95
I-80
95
93
225
93
6
93
I-15

① Buck Point.
② Rocky Point.
③ Pelican Point.
④ Boy Scout camp.
⑤ Gallatin Boat Ramp & Marina.
⑥ Boat launch.
⑦ Spaulding boat launch.
⑧ Troxel Point.

EAGLE LAKE

NOT TO SCALE

Eagle Lake

The key to fly fishing Eagle Lake is to hit it when it's ON. In this condition Eagle rates a 10 on the quality-of-fly-fishing scale. That's because it's home to the Eagle Lake rainbow, a strain of the hardiest, fastest growing trout in the West. Plus, more than 200,000 trout are planted in the lake annually. If you want to catch a giant rainbow in this part of the world, Eagle Lake is a good place to start.

This large, alkaline body of water sits in the mountains just above Susanville, California. During the warm months of summer, fish tend to stay out in deeper, colder water. But when temperatures in the shallows remain cool, like in the early part of the season (late May–early June) or October to December, fly fishing excitement builds. Large Eagle Lake rainbows make a habit of cruising near shore in search of food during these months and under these conditions. Productivity peaks at this time, rewarding fly fishers who wade along rock- or tule-lined shores or cast from boats and float tubes.

It's a good idea to target or pre-select the areas you want to fish and to get there early, or in advance of other anglers. These popular spots include the flats at the north end of Eagle Lake, around the marina at the south end of the lake, and the shorelines near Spaulding, Pelican Point, and the old Boy Scout camp (across from Pelican Point). See the accompanying map for these places and other spots to know about.

An abundance of scuds, leeches, minnows, and some aquatic insects populate the alkaline environment. They provide excellent fly fishing opportunities. Unfortunately the weather can sometimes ruin these opportunities. It can make fishing conditions difficult, if not downright nasty. If you're boating or float tubing along the shallows and the wind comes up, head for shore. If you can put up with cold and wind, however, the trout are definitely worth the effort.

Type of Fish
A pure strain of Eagle Lake rainbow trout.

Known Hatches
Not really a "hatch" lake, but there are some midges and damsels. Most fly fishers key on the scuds, leeches, and minnows.

Equipment to Use
Rods: 5–7 weight, 8'–9'.
Reels: Palm or mechanical drag.
Lines: 5–7 weight, floating or intermediate.
Leaders: Short and stout 7½', 3X or 4X.
Wading: Neoprene waders and felt-soled boots for the cold water. A float tube or boat is the best way to cover a lot of water.

Flies to Use
Dry patterns: Of little importance, possibly suspended Midge Emergers.
Nymphs: Scuds and snail patterns, Sheep Creek Special, Marabou and Mohair Leech patterns, small Olive Bird's Nest.
Streamers: Copper-brown Krystal Buggers, Gray Zonkers to imitate minnows, Staynor Ducktail.

When to Fish
Weeks after the lake opens in late May until warmwater drives fish deeper. Best from late September to close (December 31) if the water doesn't ice over.

Seasons & Limits
Saturday before Memorial Day until December 31. Verify current California Department of Fish & Game regulations.

Accommodations & Services
Plenty of motel and RV space in and around Susanville. Several very tidy campgrounds around the lake. Limited motel and eating establishments in Spaulding and other points along the shore.
Eagle Lake Marina (530) 825-3454.
Mariners Resort (800) 700-LAKE or (530) 825-3333.

Rating
A special fishery that's worth a try. When it's "happening," an easy 10. Generally an 8.5.

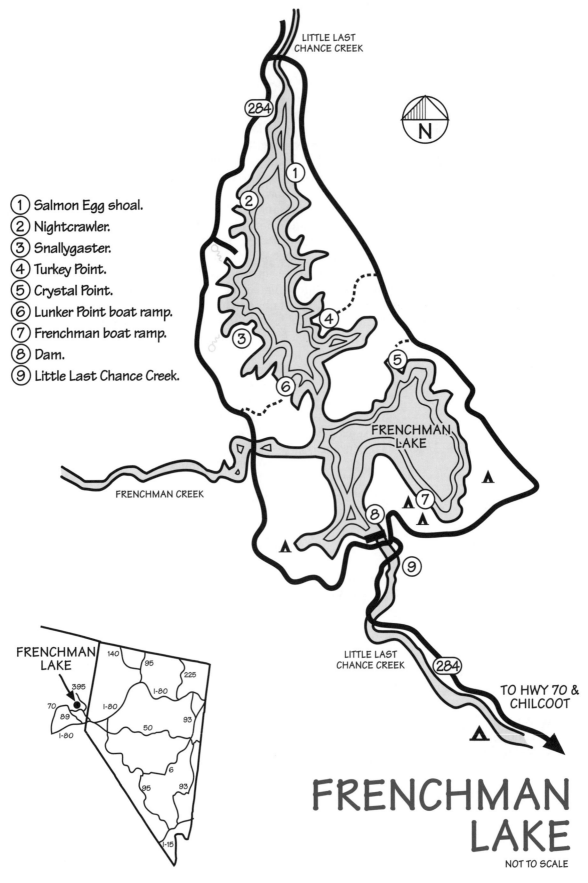

1. Salmon Egg shoal.
2. Nightcrawler.
3. Snallygaster.
4. Turkey Point.
5. Crystal Point.
6. Lunker Point boat ramp.
7. Frenchman boat ramp.
8. Dam.
9. Little Last Chance Creek.

LITTLE LAST CHANCE CREEK

FRENCHMAN LAKE

FRENCHMAN CREEK

LITTLE LAST CHANCE CREEK

284

TO HWY 70 & CHILCOOT

FRENCHMAN LAKE

NOT TO SCALE

FRENCHMAN LAKE

140
95
225
I-80
395
I-80
70
89
I-80
50
93
6
95
93
I-15

Frenchman Lake

Frenchman Lake is a deep manmade impoundment, located about 20 miles west of Davis Lake and approximately seven miles north of the town of Chilcoot, California. This is a good place to try if Davis is off. Managed as a put-and-take fishery, Frenchman receives hundreds of thousands of stockers each year. It is also subject to windy conditions and cold weather, befitting an alpine setting of more than 5,000 feet in elevation.

It's best fly fished in the large- to pocket-sized, wind-protected bays that characterize most of the shoreline. At the northern end, where the main stream enters the lake, weed beds flourish, supporting many aquatic life forms, including those of particular interest to fly fishers: damsels, snails, mayflies, and midges.

During summer months, Frenchman provides good evening surface activity when the wind cooperates. Midges are the primary hatch, and a variety of surface and suspended patterns work well. Damsel and callibaetis mayfly hatches can be very productive from late May to July and are best fished while wading or from a floating craft in 4' or less of water.

In the fall, Snails and Small Leeches can create some spectacular fly action. Fish these patterns slowly on a floating or intermediate line.

Below the dam, Little Last Chance Creek offers plenty of trout in a tailwater-type fishery. These fish have been planted, but the easy access, pretty setting, and variety of fly fishing water makes this creek worth checking out.

Type of Fish
Rainbow and brown trout.

Known Hatches
Primary hatches include "blood" midges, damsels, and callibaetis. There are some evening caddis hatches during the summer months.

Equipment to Use
Rods: 4–6 weight, 8'–9½'.
Line: Floating, 4–6 weight. Intermediate or sinking, 2–4 weight.
Leaders: Wet lines for deep water, short and stout 7½', 3X or 4X. Intermediate and dry, 9'–12', 4X–6X.
Reels: Standard trout reels are fine.
Wading: Neoprene waders and felt-soled boots for cold water. Wet-wade in warm weather. Easily fished from shore or a small boat.

Flies to Use
Dry patterns: Suspended Midge Emergers, Callibaetis Emergers, Parachutes, Damsels.
Nymphs: Snails, Sheep Creek Special, Dragonflies, Timberline Emergers, Marabou Damsel, Pheasant Tail, small Olive and Black Bird's Nest.
Streamers: Black, Gray, and Olive Leeches; Brown Woolly or Krystal Buggers.

When to Fish
The lake fishes from ice-out until mid- to late July. The very best time to fish Frenchman is from mid-September until the lake ices over.

Seasons & Limits
Frenchman is open year-round. Check current California Department of Fish & Game Regulations.

Accommodations & Services
Motel and RV spaces, as well as restaurant, laundry, and auto services, are best in and around Portola, California and 40 miles away in Reno, Nevada. There is a general store with gas in Chilcoot. Several good campgrounds around the lake are convenient.

Rating
Generally, Frenchman rates a 7 or 7.5. During the best hatch times, however, this rating increases to the 8.5 to 9 range.

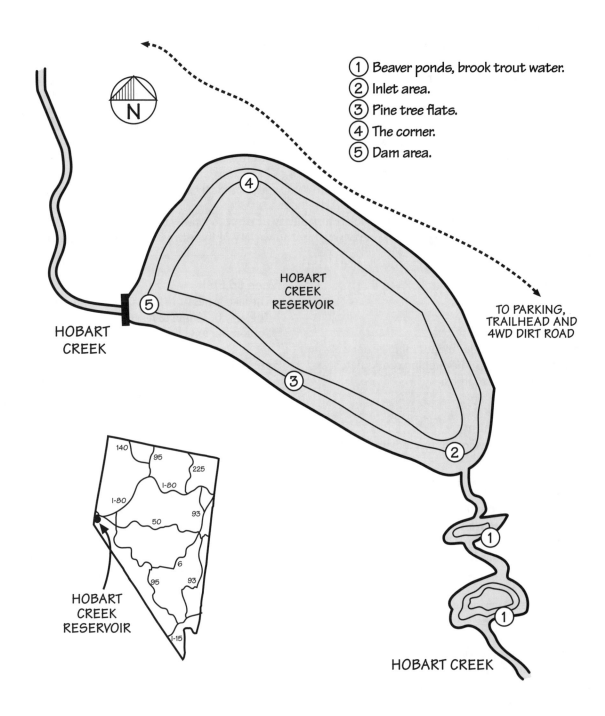

1. Beaver ponds, brook trout water.
2. Inlet area.
3. Pine tree flats.
4. The corner.
5. Dam area.

HOBART CREEK RESERVOIR

TO PARKING, TRAILHEAD AND 4WD DIRT ROAD

HOBART CREEK

HOBART CREEK RESERVOIR

HOBART CREEK

HOBART CREEK RESERVOIR

NOT TO SCALE

Hobart Creek Reservoir

This is probably the best place in the Carson City area to take children or beginning fly anglers and get them into fishing. If you want a fun and beautiful place to spend the day, try Hobart. It's only about 10 acres in surface area and 15 feet deep, and has a lot of aquatic vegetation and insect life.

Hobart Creek Reservoir sits in a wilderness area atop the mountains, at more than 7,000 feet in elevation, just west of Nevada's state capital. While the reservoir is only five short miles from Carson City, it can only be accessed by four miles of extremely rough, 4WD dirt road. This takes you to the trailhead, from which you'll have to hike for another mile and a quarter. But then you're there!

Nestled in pine, fir, willow, alder, and aspen trees, and subdivided by several beaver ponds (in the upper end), this small impoundment is one of Nevada's most beautiful still water fisheries. While Hobart is a popular weekend destination for the 4WD crowd, during the week you can often have the lake to yourself.

Trout are not big here, but what they lack in size they make up for in numbers and their willingness to take a fly. A float tube is the most enjoyable way to fish this lake, as long as you don't mind packing it in.

Believe it or not, the easy way to Hobart starts from downtown Carson City and Washington Street, right near the Nevada State Museum. Go west on Washington about half a mile until it turns into Ash Canyon Road. Take this road, which is about four miles of tedious four-wheel driving, to the trailhead. Then, hike the mile and a quarter.

Type of Fish
Hobart has literally tons of 4–10" brook trout. The populations of rainbow or cutbow trout depend on what was most recently planted by the Nevada Department of Wildlife.

Known Hatches
Excellent midge, good damsel, and sporadic mayfly hatches. One of the better flies to use here is a Mosquito pattern, which suggests one might want to also pack along some repellent.

Equipment to Use
Rods: 3–6 weight, 8½'–9'.
Line: Floating, intermediate sink or type 2 full-sink line to match the rod.
Leaders: Sinking, 6'–7½', 3X–4X.
Floating, 9'–12', 5X–7X.
Reels: Click or disk drag balanced to rod.
Wading: Use neoprene waders and felt-soled boots for the cold water. Bring your float tube and fins if you don't mind packing them in.

Flies to Use
Dry patterns: Royal Wulff, brightly colored Humpies, Elk Hair Caddis for the brookies. Otherwise, use suspended Midge patterns, Callibaetis Paranymphs, Parachute Adams, Parachute Hare's Ears, Mosquitos.

Nymphs: Scuds, Damsels, Small Peacock bodies like Zug Bug or Prince, Pheasant Tail, Bird's Nest, Hare's Ear. Soft Hackle, small Midge and Mosquito Larva and Pupa imitations.
Streamers: Olive, Brown, and Black Woolly Buggers and Leeches.

When to Fish
Fishing here is determined by accessibility. If you can get there, Hobart fishes well all summer. The water temperature stays cool because of the lake's high elevation.

Seasons & Limits
Open from May 1 to September 30. Two fish over 12". Artificial lures or flies with single barbless hooks only. Regulations can change, so check the *Nevada Fishing Regulations* booklet.

Accommodations & Services
Take whatever you need with you as there is nothing available after leaving Carson City. No camping.

Rating
Not many big fish, but abundance and "catchability" earn Hobart a 7. If you take a child with you, he or she will call the trip a 10!

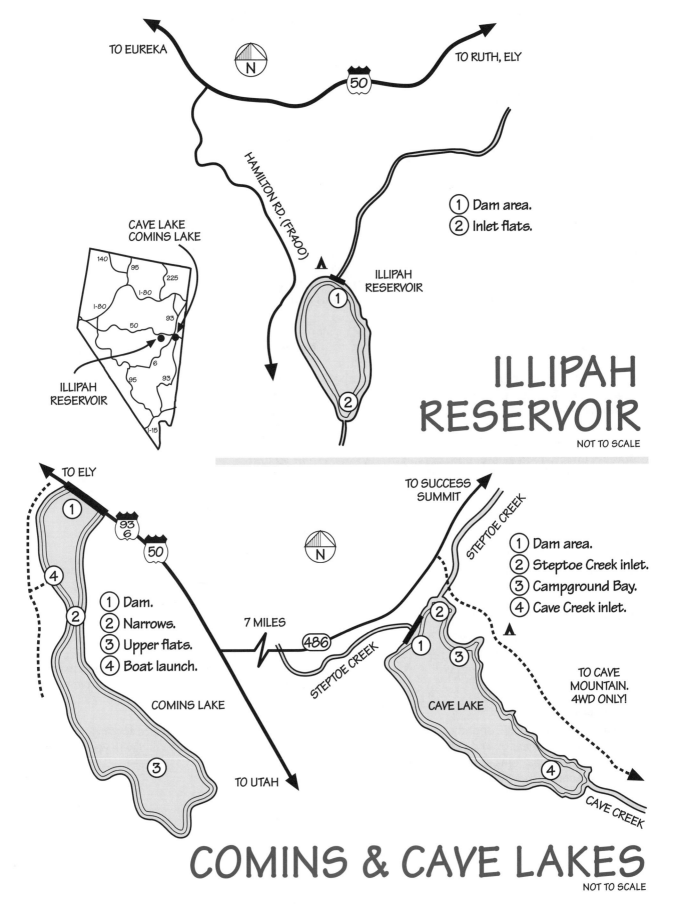

TO EUREKA

TO RUTH, ELY

50

HAMILTON RD. (FR400)

CAVE LAKE
COMINS LAKE

140 | 95
I-80 | 225
I-80
50 | 93
6
95 | 93
I-15

ILLIPAH
RESERVOIR

① Dam area.
② Inlet flats.

ILLIPAH
RESERVOIR

① Dam area

ILLIPAH RESERVOIR

NOT TO SCALE

TO ELY

①
93
6
50
④
②

① Dam.
② Narrows.
③ Upper flats.
④ Boat launch.

COMINS LAKE

③

7 MILES

486

STEPTOE CREEK

TO SUCCESS
SUMMIT

STEPTOE CREEK

① Dam area.
② Steptoe Creek inlet.
③ Campground Bay.
④ Cave Creek inlet.

②
①
③

CAVE LAKE

④

TO CAVE
MOUNTAIN.
4WD ONLY!

CAVE CREEK

TO UTAH

COMINS & CAVE LAKES

NOT TO SCALE

Illipah Reservoir, Comins Lake, & Cave Lake

While the town of Ely, in eastern Nevada, is best known for its elk herd and incredibly cold temperatures during the winter months, the area offers some exceptional fly fishing opportunities.

Illipah Reservoir is located in the White Pine Range, 35 miles west of Ely, and sits in the high desert at 6,770 feet in elevation. Illipah is small, around 70 acres, and is managed by the Nevada Department of Wildlife as a put-and-take fishery. The reservoir is stocked in spring and fall with 8" to 10" rainbow and brown trout. During good water years the reservoir is 50 feet deep at the dam and holdover fish from previous seasons grow large. Angler success is generally good here except during the hottest summer weather.

Comins Lake has gained the reputation of Nevada's newest "superstar" still water. Located about five miles south of Ely on Highway 50 in Steptoe Valley, this lake is easy to access and fish both from shore and in float tubes and boats. A good source of cold water, combined with an excellent biomass, provide Comins with the perfect conditions for healthy fish that grow very fast. Rainbow and brown trout of four pounds or more are not uncommon here. The Nevada Department of Wildlife plans to expand the size of the Comins in the near future, which should provide even more quality fly fishing for anglers exploring this part of the state.

Cave Lake serves as the centerpiece of Cave Lake State Park. It is situated in alpine terrain at 7,300 feet in elevation in the Schell Creek Range. Cave Lake covers 32 surface acres and reaches 60 feet in depth behind the dam. Brook, rainbow, and brown trout are all present in the reservoir, and while the average fish is less than 12", one Cave Lake brown weighed 27 pounds, 5 ounces. It was caught in 1984 and as of this writing, still stands as the Nevada state record.

Although these three still waters offer limited dry fly action, anglers Midge fishing with Indicators, swimming Nymphs in and around the weed beds, and searching the depths with Buggers, Leeches, and Streamers will find plenty of willing trout to make the trip to Ely worthwhile.

Types of Fish
Stocked rainbows and smaller populations of brown trout. Brook trout in Cave Lake.

Known Hatches
Damselflies, dragonflies, mayflies, and midges.

Equipment to Use
Rods: 4–6 weight 8'–9'.
Lines: Floating, intermediate and II sink, to match rod.
Leaders: Sinking line, 6'– 7 ½', 3X–5X.
Floating line, 9'–12', 4X–6X.
Reels: Click or disk drag to balance rod.
Wading: Hippers for shore fishing. Float tubes or a boat work best.

Flies to Use
Dry patterns: Small suspended Midge patterns, Callibaetis Duns, Adult Damsels.
Nymphs: Zug Bug, Prince, Brassies, Black and Olive Bird's Nest, Hare's Ear, Soft Hackle and small Pheasant Tail (greased, fished just under the surface), Midge Larva or Pupa patterns, Damsel and Dragon patterns, Snail, Scuds.

Streamers: Olive, Brown, or Black Woolly Bugger and Leech patterns, Staynor Ducktail, Sheep Creek Special, Marabous, especially black.

When to Fish
Except for the hottest day in summer, these lakes fish well April–October.

Seasons and Limits
All are open year-round, day and night. Limits vary, so check current Nevada Department of Wildlife regulations. All freeze over in winter.

Accommodations and Services
Closest full services are in Ely. Illipah has a no-fee campground: tables, fire pits, toilets, unimproved boat launch. Cave Lake, a state park, has two fee campgrounds with flush toilets, showers, picnic, and day-use facilities. Comins Lake is a day-use area with toilets and an unimproved boat launch.

Rating
Cave Lake rates a 7, Illipah an 8, and Comins a solid 9.

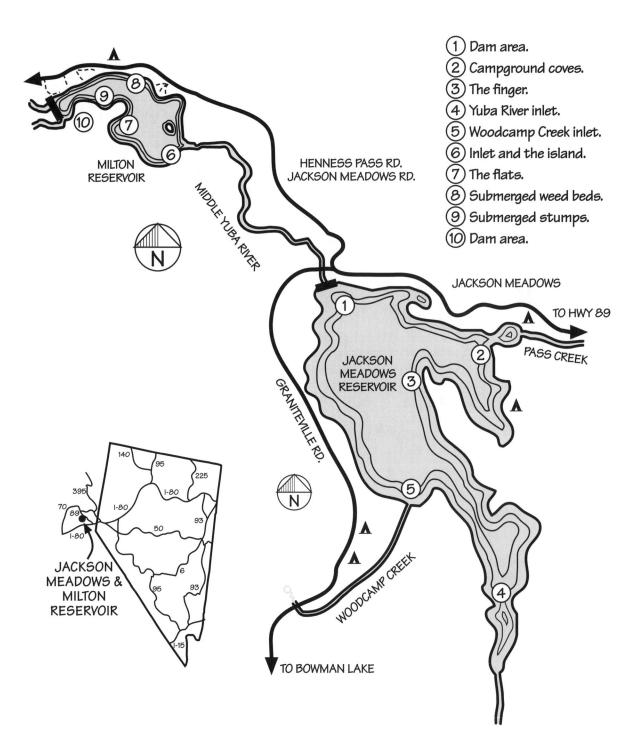

1. Dam area.
2. Campground coves.
3. The finger.
4. Yuba River inlet.
5. Woodcamp Creek inlet.
6. Inlet and the island.
7. The flats.
8. Submerged weed beds.
9. Submerged stumps.
10. Dam area.

JACKSON MEADOWS & MILTON RESERVIORS

NOT TO SCALE

Jackson Meadows & Milton Reservoirs

Jackson Meadows, at more than 6,000 feet in elevation, provides a typical picturesque and forested Sierra Nevada mountain lake. An additional benefit is that it's easy to get to. Located 25 miles north of Truckee, California (most take Highway 89 north), the reservoir is a convenient staging area for backpackers and others heading into the forest. Don't let this deter you. This drive-up convenience is a plus for the fly fisher.

A boat or float tube is necessary on most of the water due to the steep nature of the banks. But you won't have to pack it very far. The lake has a boat ramp and several access areas for tubers. The best fly fishing area is the upper end, where the Middle Yuba River enters the reservoir. Fishing the evening midge hatch is most productive for fly casters.

Milton is a small, 70-acre reservoir located one and a half miles below the Jackson Meadows dam. Milton is even prettier than Jackson: one of the most scenic still waters in the eastern Sierra. It can also be a very productive fly fishing spot as well.

The water at Milton is very clear and cold most of the season. Presentation and fly selection here are at a premium because cruising trout, particularly in the shallows, can be very selective. Dry fly activity is excellent early and late in the season.

The Middle Yuba River, which connects the two reservoirs, is also a fun and challenging fishery during the summer months. Both reservoirs are planted with rainbow trout each year.

Type of Fish

Both lakes hold healthy populations of rainbow and brown trout, with the occasional cutthroat.

Known Hatches

Midges, all year. Callibaetis, May and September. Damsel migrations June and July. *Siphlonurus* (grey drakes) in early June on Milton. Flying ants in June, evening caddis all summer.

Equipment to Use

Rods: 3–6 weight, 8½'–9'.
Line: Floating, Intermediate sink, or type II full-sink line to match the rod.
Leaders: Sinking lines: 6'–7½', 3X–4X.
Floating lines: 9'–12', 5X–7X.
Reels: Click or disk drag balanced to rod.
Wading: Chest-high neoprenes and felt-soled boots. Limited wading at Jackson Meadows due to steep banks. Wade flats at Milton. A float tube or boat works well on both.

Flies to Use

Dry patterns: Suspended Midge, Callibaetis Paranymph, Parachute Adams. Summer evenings try small Caddis.

Nymphs: Damsel, Pheasant Tail, Hare's Ear, midge larva imitations like Brassies, Small Bird's Nest.
Streamers: Olive, Brown, and Black Woolly Buggers and Leeches, baitfish imitations, Matukas, and Zonkers.

When to Fish

Late May to early August, and from mid-September to October.

Seasons & Limits

Open the last Saturday in April to November 15. Jackson Meadows has general limits and regulations. Milton has a two fish under 12" limit and single barbless hook regulations. Always check a copy of *California Sport Fishing Regulations*.

Accommodations & Services

Closest services are 25 miles away in Truckee, California. There are improved Forest Service campgrounds at Jackson Meadows and free, first-come, first-serve, camping spots at Milton.

Rating

Jackson Meadows a 5. Milton an 8 or 9.

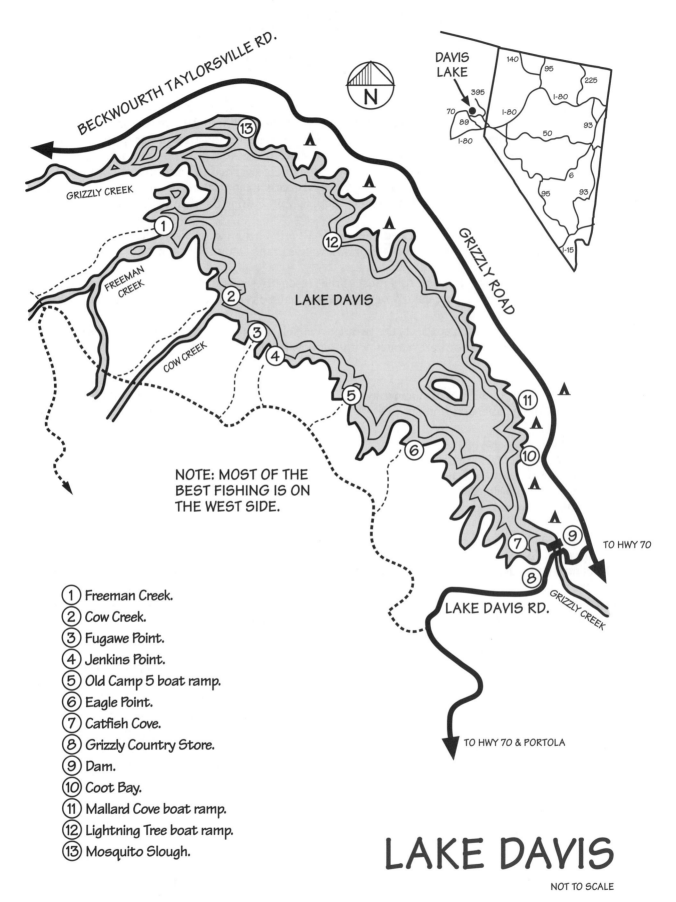

NOTE: MOST OF THE BEST FISHING IS ON THE WEST SIDE.

1. Freeman Creek.
2. Cow Creek.
3. Fugawe Point.
4. Jenkins Point.
5. Old Camp 5 boat ramp.
6. Eagle Point.
7. Catfish Cove.
8. Grizzly Country Store.
9. Dam.
10. Coot Bay.
11. Mallard Cove boat ramp.
12. Lightning Tree boat ramp.
13. Mosquito Slough.

LAKE DAVIS

NOT TO SCALE

Lake Davis

There's nothing quite like fly fishing Lake Davis mid-June through July, when the damsels are out and about. This one-of-a-kind experience gets a perfect 10 rating. During other months of the season, the fishery scores an 8.5.

Lake Davis is about 50 miles north of Reno and seven miles north of Portola, California, in the northeastern part of the state. The lake (reservoir) was built as a water supply for this small town, hence there's no swimming, water skiing, jet skiing, or other forms of motorized mayhem. This is a blessing for anyone who has struggled to fish waters where these multiple-use activities take place.

Lake Davis is not particularly deep, except near the dam. The majority of water can be fly fished effectively, especially around the huge, lush weed beds. These sprout up during the summer months along the western shore. Try from Eagle Point along the northwest banks up to Mosquito Slough and where Freeman and Grizzly creeks enter the lake.

The Davis weed beds support healthy populations of snails, scuds, damsels, dragons, midges, mayflies, caddisflies, leeches, and baitfish. There are even stoneflies near the creek mouths and a fairly predictable carpenter ant "hatch" in late May and June.

Large midge and caddis hatches are common at Davis. When the fish are "on" these bugs, fishing can be exceptional. In the fall Davis becomes much less crowded, and casting to hungry, cruising trout in the shallows is very productive.

Despite the bountiful bugs, the most exciting time to fish Davis is during the damsel migration. This generally begins in mid-June and often lasts until the end of July. At this time large rainbows, up to seven pounds, come to the surface and into the shallows to slash greedily among hundreds of thousands of damsel nymphs as the insects are making their way to shore. It's not uncommon to hook the trout of the summer, or even of a lifetime, in less than two feet of water!

In recent years, illegal introductions of northern pike have adversely affected the trout fishery. The California Department of Fish & Game continues to try to solve this problem.

Type of Fish
Primarily rainbow trout. Also some browns and growing populations of illegally stocked largemouth bass and northern pike.

Known Hatches
Because of the extensive and varied biomass of Davis, there is not room to list all known hatches. The lake is best fished with surface flies during the summer "blood" midge emergence, callibaetis hatch and the world-class damsel migration.

Equipment to Use
Rods: 4–6 weight, 8½'–9'.
Reels: Palm or mechanical drag.
Line: Floating, 4–6 weight. Intermediate, sinking 2–4.
Leaders: For deep wet lines, 7½', 3X–4X. Intermediate and dry lines, 9'–12', 4X–6X.
Wading: Neoprene waders and felt-soled boots for cold water. Otherwise, wet-wade or use a boat or float tube.

Flies to Use
Dry patterns: Suspended Midge and Callibaetis emergers, Parachute Adams, dry Damsel patterns, small Caddis.

Nymphs: Snail patterns, Sheep Creek Special, Dragonfly Nymph, Marabou Damsel, Pheasant Tail, small Olive and Black Bird's Nest, Blood Midge pupa.
Streamers: Leech patterns such as Black, Olive, or Brown Woolly or Krystal Buggers.

When to Fish
If the lake is accessible, ice-out is an excellent time to fish Davis, as is mid-June through July and again from mid-September until the lake ices over.

Seasons & Limits
Open year-round. Limits can change; check the *California Sport Fishing Regulations* booklet and ask at a local fly shop.

Accommodations & Services
Motel and RV spaces, as well as restaurant, laundry, and auto services are in and around Portola, California. Several very good campgrounds and a general store are at the lake. Grizzly Country Store, (916) 832-0270.

Rating
Year in and year out, one of the eastern Sierra's best fisheries. During the damsel migration, Davis is a solid 10. The rest of the year, it's an 8.5, or maybe even a 9.

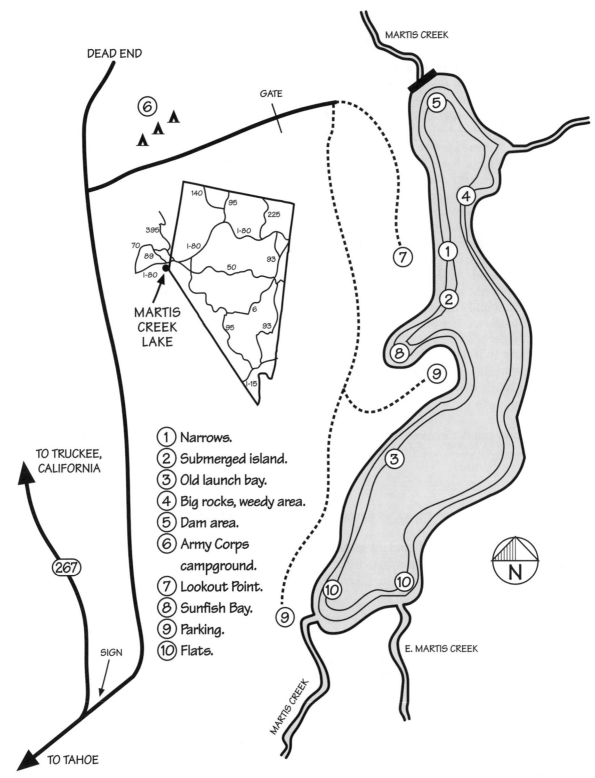

DEAD END

MARTIS CREEK

GATE

① Narrows.
② Submerged island.
③ Old launch bay.
④ Big rocks, weedy area.
⑤ Dam area.
⑥ Army Corps campground.
⑦ Lookout Point.
⑧ Sunfish Bay.
⑨ Parking.
⑩ Flats.

TO TRUCKEE, CALIFORNIA

267

SIGN

TO TAHOE

MARTIS CREEK LAKE

MARTIS CREEK

E. MARTIS CREEK

N

NOT TO SCALE

Martis Creek Lake

At minimum pool, Martis is a basic 70-acre lake built by the Army Corps of Engineers for flood control. Then it was selected as the first still water for California's Wild Trout Program. Since 1979 "no boat motors" (either gas or electric) and strict catch and release rules have helped grow fine trout in this lake. Regulations also mandate use of single barbless hooks. Cutthroat trout, which flourished in the 1980s, are now all but gone, replaced by good populations of rainbows and browns.

Located only about four miles south of Truckee, California, Martis is an extremely easy lake to get to and enjoy. In recent years fluctuating water levels and unknown factors have affected trout growth and survival here. We hope that ongoing efforts by the California Department of Fish & Game will reverse this trend in the near future. Nevertheless this is a convenient "after work" fly fishing outing for many Reno, Truckee, and Lake Tahoe area locals.

Martis Creek Reservoir is barely 25 feet deep at minimum pool. It has large numbers of green sunfish and other minnows as well as a good crayfish population. Using a fast sinking line or shooting head with these imitations can produce surprising results. During non-hatch periods, fishing a Blood Midge Pupa 3'–6' under an indicator will often provide strikes.

Martis Creek, which flows into the reservoir, is a rainbow and brown trout spawning stream and is closed to all fishing. The outflow stream is a spawning tributary to the Truckee River and can produce some big trout early in the season. Please practice catch and release if you fish this stream.

Summer algae blooms and heavy weed growth have diminished angler success during July, August, and early September. Martis fishes best early in the season and in the fall.

Type of Fish

Primarily rainbow and brown trout. There are probably still some cutthroat left from the reservoir's initial population. Also, illegally introduced green sunfish.

Known Hatches

Callibaetis, small mayflies, damselflies, and midges. The most important midge is the giant blood midge. Caddis during the summer evenings. Some little yellow stoneflies near the mouths of the two creeks that feed the reservoir.

Equipment to Use

Rods: 3–6 weight, 8½'–9'.
Line: Floating, Intermediate sink, and type II full-sink lines to match rod.
Leaders: Sinking, 6'–7', 3X–4X. Floating, 9'–12', 5X–7X.
Reels: Click or disk drag balanced to rod.
Wading: Neoprene waders and felt-soled boots during cold weather. Wet-wade during warm weather. Generally wading is limited in the lake. A float tube or pram is very handy here.

Flies to Use

Dry patterns: Suspended Midge patterns, especially the Giant Blood Midge, Callibaetis Paranymphs, Elk Hair Caddis, Parachute Adams, and Parachute Hare's Ears. Adult Damsels, Spent Rusty Spinners, and small Caddis.
Nymphs: Damsel, Pheasant Tail, Hare's Ear, Blood Midge pupa. Brassies and imitations of small Midge Larva and Pupas. Soft Hackle flies also work well.

Streamers: Olive and Black Woolly Buggers and Leeches. In fall, use large Brown Woolly Buggers to imitate the abundant crayfish population, Olive Matukas and Zonkers to imitate baitfish.

When to Fish

Spring and fall are the best times to fish Martis, especially during the predictable evening hatches of blood midges. Early spring runoff can cause the water level to rise and affect the fly fishing. The dog days of mid-July to mid-September are less productive and are best fished with a fast-sinking line in deeper water.

Seasons & Limits

Open the last Saturday in April until November 15. Barbless, artificial lures only; catch and release. All tributaries are closed all year. Check current California regulations.

Accommodations & Services

Closest services are four miles away at either the Northstar Resort or in Truckee, California, or 16 miles over the pass in King's Beach, at the edge of Lake Tahoe. There is an excellent improved campground one-half mile above Martis. Run by the Corps of Engineers, it takes campers on a first-come, first-served basis.

Rating

The fly fishing generally rates a 5. Evening blood midge hatches often produce some good dry fly activity, and the occasional monster trout is still dredged from the depths.

39

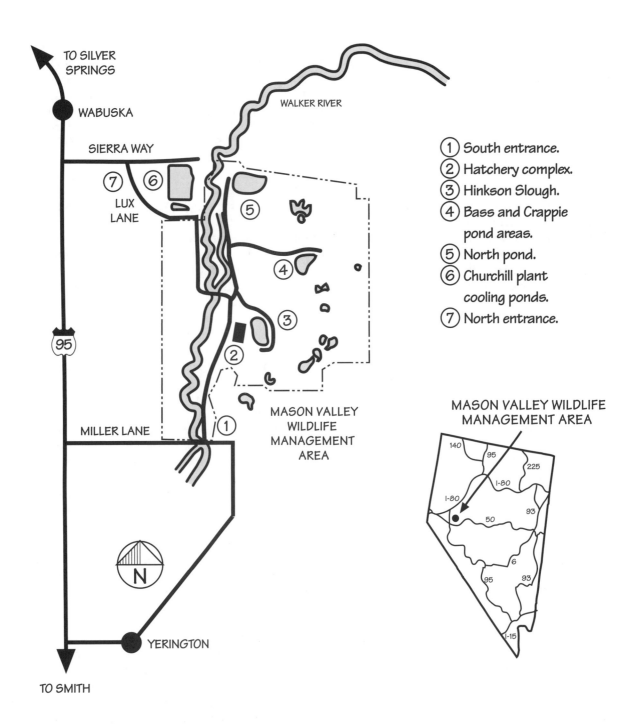

TO SILVER SPRINGS

WABUSKA

SIERRA WAY

⑦ ⑥

LUX LANE

⑤

WALKER RIVER

④

③

②

①

95

MILLER LANE

N

YERINGTON

TO SMITH

① South entrance.
② Hatchery complex.
③ Hinkson Slough.
④ Bass and Crappie pond areas.
⑤ North pond.
⑥ Churchill plant cooling ponds.
⑦ North entrance.

MASON VALLEY WILDLIFE MANAGEMENT AREA

MASON VALLEY WILDLIFE MANAGEMENT AREA

140
95
225
I-80
I-80
I-80
50
93
6
95
93
I-15

MASON VALLEY WILDLIFE MANAGEMENT AREA

NOT TO SCALE

Mason Valley Wildlife Management Area

Whether you're after bass or trout, the Mason Valley Wildlife Management Area offers a top-rated opportunity to catch sizable fish with a fly rod. Located just outside Yerington, Nevada, this 13,000-acre ranch is managed by the Nevada Department of Wildlife for waterfowl, deer, turkey, pheasant, quail, bass, and trout, among other wildlife. The trout grow fast here and the bass are plentiful.

There are a total of 36 ponds in the wildlife area. Only four (Hinkson Slough, Bass Pond, Crappie Pond, and North Pond) are open to fishing. The other 32 ponds are closed to all trespass to permit undisturbed waterfowl nesting and rearing during spring and summer.

Trout anglers will want to concentrate on Hinkson Slough, a 45-acre pond east of the state fish hatchery. Cold groundwater pumped through the hatchery dumps into this impoundment, providing trout with comfortable habitat, even during the hot summer months.

As "slough" suggests, Hinkson is marshy and shallow, about 6 to 8 feet at its deepest. There are lots of tules and dark-colored water conditions not usually associated with a trophy trout fishery. This discolored water however, is a veritable stew pot of vegetation and insect life. Huge midge hatches often blanket the water. Fishing a dry line, a greased leader, or an indicator with a midge pupa can be deadly.

Bass Pond and Crappie Pond are medium-sized marshes with excellent largemouth habitat. Fish are plentiful and some are quite big. From April through late summer they are eager to take a well-presented fly. Bass will usually charge to the surface to smash poppers or divers. North Pond was completed in 1998. This 190-acre impoundment provides additional bass fishing on par with the other lakes in Mason Valley WMA.

Adjacent to the north end of Mason Valley Wildlife Management Area is Churchill Power Plant and its related cooling ponds. The "Ponds" are used to cool and recirculate water used in the electrical generation process. The warmwater discharged from the plant helps create good bass habitat. No boats or float tubes are allowed, so fish here while walking the rocky shoreline.

Type of Fish
Rainbow, brown, and cuttbow trout; largemouth bass and sunfish.

Known Hatches
Hatches are giant in terms of numbers and sizes of insects. Look for midges as well as decent callibaetis and damsel activity.

Equipment to Use
Rods: Trout, 4–6 weight, 8½'–9'. Bass, 6–7 weight.
Reels: Click or disk to balance rod.
Line: Floating or intermediate sink matched to the rod.
Leaders: Sinking, 6'–7½', 3X–4X. Floating, 9'–12', 4X–6X.
Wading: Much of this area is not conducive to wading. It's best fished from a float tube or small pram. Wear waders to fish from the pond edges and dikes.

Flies to Use
Dry patterns: Giant and smaller suspended Midges, Callibaetis Paranymphs, Parachute Adams, Parachute Hare's Ears. Believe it or not, for some spectacular fishing after dark, use floating Black-Foam Zonkers.
Nymphs for trout: Soft Hackle, small Pheasant Tail (greased and fished just under the surface); Brassie #10–20; Midge Larva or Pupas, Black Bird's Nest; Damselflies and Dragonflies, Snail, Small Peacock-Body Zug Bug, Prince.

Streamers for trout: Olive, Brown, and Black Woolly Buggers and Leeches, Staynor Ducktail, Sheep Creek Special, or Muddler Minnow greased and fished just under the surface.
Bass: Assorted divers, streamers, Woolly Buggers, poppers, and Frogs.

When to Fish
The best time for trout is from opening day through March. Trout fishing drops off in April and early May, but bass fishing kicks in. From late May through September, trout fishing can be good in the mornings, late evenings, and after dark. You'll have to pick your spots due to heavy weed buildup.

Seasons & Limits
Second Saturday in February to September 30. Artificial lures or flies with single barbless hooks only. Check current regulations.

Accommodations & Services
All services eight miles away in Yerington, Nevada.

Rating
Early in the season, Hinkson is a solid 8. The rest of the year it rates a 7 for trout. Bass fishing at Mason Valley rates an 8.5 from April on. If you work hard and get a lot of fish, it's a 10.

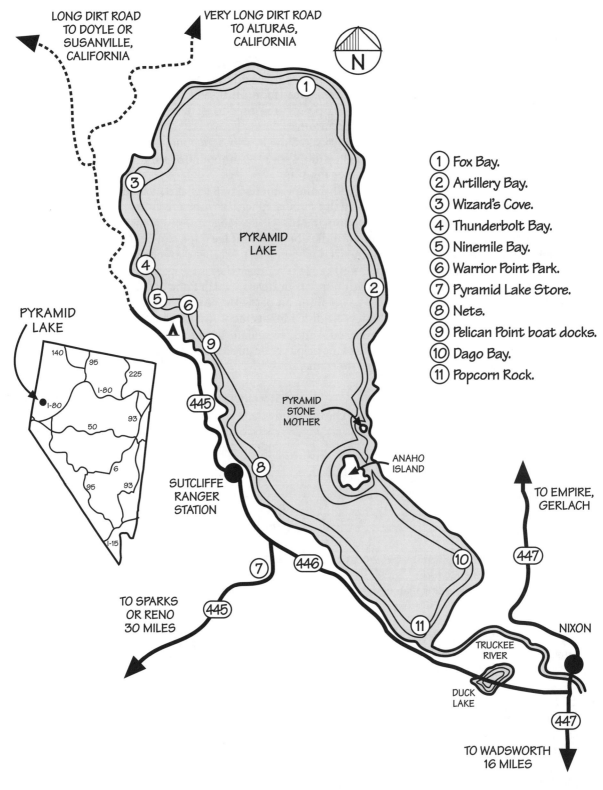

LONG DIRT ROAD TO DOYLE OR SUSANVILLE, CALIFORNIA

VERY LONG DIRT ROAD TO ALTURAS, CALIFORNIA

N

PYRAMID LAKE

1 — Fox Bay.
2 — Artillery Bay.
3 — Wizard's Cove.
4 — Thunderbolt Bay.
5 — Ninemile Bay.
6 — Warrior Point Park.
7 — Pyramid Lake Store.
8 — Nets.
9 — Pelican Point boat docks.
10 — Dago Bay.
11 — Popcorn Rock.

PYRAMID LAKE

140
95
225
I-80
I-80
50
93
6
95
93
I-15

PYRAMID STONE MOTHER

ANAHO ISLAND

445

SUTCLIFFE RANGER STATION

TO EMPIRE, GERLACH

447

7   446

445

TO SPARKS OR RENO 30 MILES

10

11

NIXON

TRUCKEE RIVER

DUCK LAKE

447

TO WADSWORTH 16 MILES

PYRAMID LAKE

NOT TO SCALE

Pyramid Lake

What angler worth his or her salt has not heard of the ladder fishermen of Pyramid Lake and the trophy-sized cutthroats they cast to? This is the world's best trophy cutthroat fishery. Many also know the best time to fish this world-class lake is in the winter. If you're willing to pay your dues and can withstand the punishing cold weather, you're in for a 10 experience. The stark, desolate surroundings give you the impression you are fishing on the lunar surface or a Star Trek set.

Cold weather and cold water inspire a unique Pyramid Lake fishing technique. Neoprene-clad fly rodders usually want to get their bodies out of the frigid water and above the rolling surf. A stepladder or milk crate comes in handy. These devices, snuggled into the lake bed, also elevate the hands above the water. This facilitates the downward pulls necessary for a good double-haul cast. In short, you want to cast far out into the lake from a warmer, elevated position. This platform also gives you a better view of the rolling desert hills and jagged cliffs that ring this huge lake. On the water, giant moonlike rock formations seem to be sailing along the watery horizon. The trophy trout lurking below the waterline are what makes the place famous.

The Lahontan cutthroat trout is an inland lake dweller that eats other fish almost exclusively. In Pyramid these are mostly cui-cui and tui chubs. Feeding on these little fish, the cuts grow to impressive size. Ten to 15 pounders are common here.

More often than not, these big trout are interested in big flies. The local favorites include an assortment of different-colored Woolly Buggers and Woolly Worms (see below). Try a dark pattern like black, purple, olive, or brown as the point fly. Then use a white, chartreuse, or fluorescent pink Woolly Worm or Foam-Backed Beetle as a dropper. Minnow patterns also work well in the fall, as do Dragonfly Nymphs in the spring. A relatively new technique at Pyramid Lake is to fish two bead head nymphs under an indicator. This is especially effective during the spring spawn when large numbers of fish are in the shallows.

The farther you can cast your rig, the better off you'll be. Shooting head lines will help get the job done. The wind blows frequently here. Consequently, Pyramid Lake regulars often opt for a heavier rod than used for normal trout fishing. If you hook one of the lake's monsters, you'll be glad you have it. For more in depth information consult a copy of *Terry Barron's No Nonsense Guide to Fly Fishing Pyramid Lake*.

Type of Fish
Lahontan cutthroat trout, Sacramento perch, cui-cui, and huge populations of tui chub.

Known Hatches & Baitfish
The cui-cui and tui chub are game fish food at Pyramid. Damselflies, dragonflies, and scant midge hatches.

Equipment to Use
Rods: 6–10 weight, 9'–10'.
Reels: Click or disk drag balanced to rod.
Line: Type IV to VI shooting head, one line weight heavier than indicated on the rod.
Leaders: 6'–7 ½', 0X–3X, usually with a dropper.
Wading: Use neoprene chest or other insulated waders to ward off the cold water, and wading boots for traction.
Special gear: Short stepladder or milk crate, gloves, hat.
Equipment care: While not as salty as the ocean, the water in Pyramid is very alkaline and hard on equipment, especially reels. Rinse reels with fresh water after fishing. Rub down fly rods with a cloth dampened with fresh water.

Flies to Use
Nymphs: Dark Olive Dragonflies are a proven pattern at Pyramid, but it's best to go with streamers during fall and winter. In spring, place bead headed nymphs such as Copper Johns, Pheasant Tails, and Aggravators #10-14, under an indicator.

Streamers: In order of effectiveness: Black, Purple, Olive, and Brown Woolly Buggers and Woolly Worms, usually with red tails. These have caught more large fish at Pyramid than all other flies combined. For a dropper try a white, chartreuse, or fluorescent pink Woolly Worm, or Foam-Backed Beetles in a variety of colors.

When to Fish
Generally, fish Pyramid from Thanksgiving to Christmas for *more* fish. After President's Day weekend through April, and even into May, go for *large* fish.

Seasons & Limits
Open from October 1 to June 30. Consult Paiute Tribe for permit information. Check current regulations.

Accommodations & Services
All accommodations and services available in nearby Sutcliffe, Nixon, and Fernley, Nevada. Reno is only 40 miles away. There is a $5.00 per day fee for camping.

Rating
All-round, this fishery rates an 8 up to a 10.

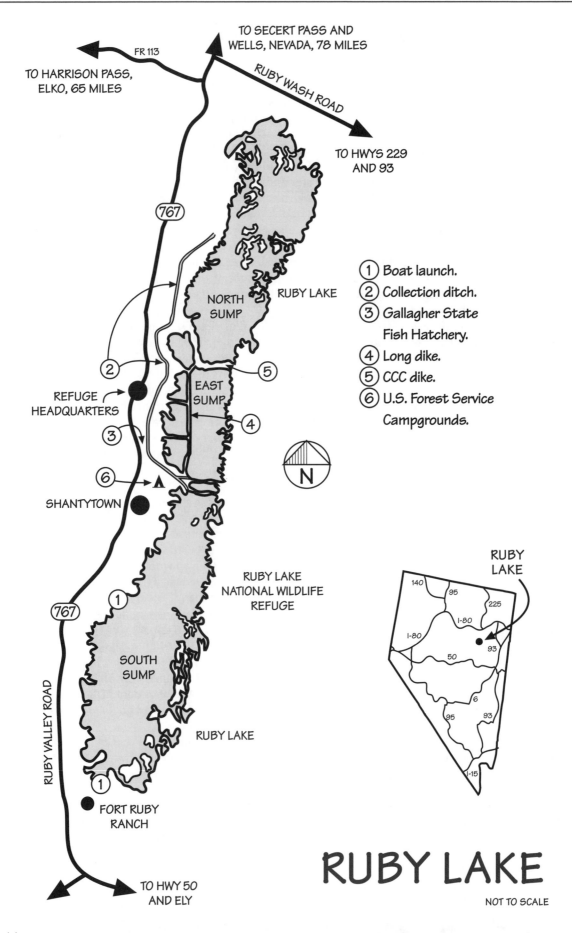

TO SECERT PASS AND
WELLS, NEVADA, 78 MILES

FR 113

TO HARRISON PASS,
ELKO, 65 MILES

RUBY WASH ROAD

TO HWYS 229
AND 93

767

NORTH
SUMP

RUBY LAKE

① Boat launch.
② Collection ditch.
③ Gallagher State
   Fish Hatchery.
④ Long dike.
⑤ CCC dike.
⑥ U.S. Forest Service
   Campgrounds.

② ⑤

REFUGE
HEADQUARTERS

EAST
SUMP

③ ④

⑥

SHANTYTOWN

N

RUBY LAKE
NATIONAL WILDLIFE
REFUGE

①

767

RUBY VALLEY ROAD

SOUTH
SUMP

RUBY LAKE

①

FORT RUBY
RANCH

TO HWY 50
AND ELY

RUBY
LAKE

140 · 95 · 225 · I-80 · I-80 · 50 · 93 · 6 · 95 · 93 · I-15

RUBY LAKE

NOT TO SCALE

Ruby Lake
National Wildlife Refuge

If you choose not to sample the excellent fly fishing at the Ruby marshes, the natural beauty of the place is reason enough to make the trip. This wonderful wetlands is populated with deer, eagles, herons, swans, geese, and every kind of duck imaginable. All of this sits at the base of the snow-topped Ruby Mountains. It's a compelling place that makes you want to return.

Located about 70 miles south of Elko, Nevada, Ruby Lake is a classic marsh, fed by a single ditch. The ditch connects a series of springs that, amazingly, provide the only source of water for several thousand acres of habitat. The Collection Ditch, as it's called, amounts to a man-made spring creek. The federal hatchery on the refuge keeps this water well supplied with trout. Many are in the trophy class and are available year-round.

The water in the marsh fluctuates from year to year depending on the level of the groundwater that feeds the springs. At 6,000 feet in elevation, the Ruby Valley keeps air and water temperatures relatively cool. This provides excellent conditions for trout as well as a growing population of largemouth bass.

For trout, fish the deeper holding waters by stripping streamers, Woolly Worms, and damsel patterns. Many sections of the Collection Ditch are shallow, and you can see the cruising trout (and they can see you). To sight-fish successfully, approach the bank in a crouched position. Cast a parachute pattern with a #16–18 nymph or scud attached to the bend of your dry fly hook using 1'–2' of tippet material. The parachute will entice strikes and serve as an indicator when a fish takes the nymph.

When the bass fishing is "on" here, it's a lot of fun. The short growing season at this high elevation, however, doesn't produce big bass. Poppers and other surface patterns work well early and late in the day. Big Marabou Leeches and Woolly Buggers (especially in black or purple) will entice bass out of the thick tule cover, as will Dragonfly and Damsel Nymphs.

Type of Fish
Rainbow, brown, brook, cutthroat, and cutbow trout as well as largemouth bass.

Known Hatches
Damsels, mayflies, and midges.

Equipment to Use
Rods: 8½'–9', 4–6 weight.
Reels: Click or disk drag to balance rod.
Lines: Floating, intermediate, and II sink lines.
Leaders: Floating 9'–12', 4X–6X. Sinking 6'–7 ½', 3X–5X.
Wading: You may not wade the Collection Ditch. Fish from shore along the ditch and from dikes that crisscross most of the marsh. Boats and float tubes are allowed in certain areas. They're subject to regulations protecting waterfowl nesting areas.

Flies to Use
Trout
Dry patterns: Small suspended Midges, Parachute Adams, Adult Damsels.
Nymphs: Soft Hackle #16–18 Pheasant Tail, Midge larva or pupa like Brassie, Black Bird's Nest, Hare's Ear. Damselflies, and Dragonfly, Snail, Scud, Small Peacock-Body Zug Bug, or Prince.
Streamers: Olive, Brown, or Black Woolly Buggers, Leeches, Staynor Ducktail, Sheep Creek Special, Marabou Streamers, especially black.
Bass
Top water: Assorted poppers and Dahlberg Divers.
Streamers: Black, or Brown Bear Hair Streamers, Woolly Buggers, big Marabou Streamers.

When to Fish
Spring and fall are the best times for trout. Fish for bass from late spring through summer into early fall. Winter fishing in the Collection Ditch and spring ponds can be good, weather permitting.

Seasons & Limits
Open year-round. The Collection Ditch is restricted to artificial flies and lures with a single barbless hook. Check current regulations.

Accommodations & Services
There is a campground and general store in Shantytown, at the Ruby Marshes. Complete services in Elko, Nevada.

Rating
The fishing may vary, but the sheer joy of fishing such a beautiful place keeps it high on the list. At any given time, a solid 8.

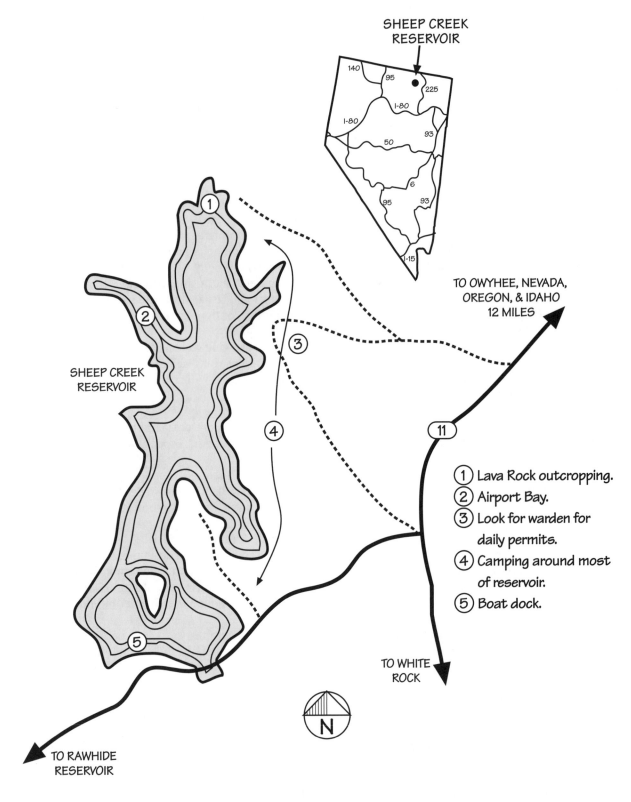

SHEEP CREEK
RESERVOIR

SHEEP CREEK
RESERVOIR

TO OWYHEE, NEVADA,
OREGON, & IDAHO
12 MILES

11

① Lava Rock outcropping.
② Airport Bay.
③ Look for warden for
   daily permits.
④ Camping around most
   of reservoir.
⑤ Boat dock.

TO WHITE
ROCK

N

TO RAWHIDE
RESERVOIR

SHEEP CREEK RESERVOIR

NOT TO SCALE

46

Sheep Creek Reservoir

How often do you have the opportunity to fish a water that gave its name to one of the most productive still water fly patterns in the West? If you take secondary State Route 11 southwest out of Owyhee for about 12 miles, you will arrive at Sheep Creek Reservoir...yes, you guessed it...home of the Sheep Creek Special.

This fly has become a still water legend. At times, the fishing at this fairly typical high desert reservoir can be legendary as well. According to float tubing author Marv Taylor, Sheep Creek was once touted as Nevada's "top rainbow fishery...with catches of 14" to 20" rainbows almost a sure thing."

This shallow body of water is situated on and controlled by the Duck Valley Indian Reservation of the Shoshone-Paiute tribes. Periodically, the reservoir has become infested with trash fish. It was poisoned a few years ago by the tribe. Now Sheep Creek is fishing as well as it has in several years. Try Airport Bay, and the old creek channel that cuts through the weed beds in the north end of the reservoir.

The reservoir is ideal for float tubing. It's only 22 feet deep and about 1,000 surface acres. Weed growth in the warmer months gets heavy. Therefore it's best to fish from ice-out to the first part of July and then again in the fall after the weeds have been knocked down by cold desert nights.

In general, the smaller stocked trout prefer mayflies, midges, small nymphs, and scuds. The large whoppers are caught on Sheep Creek Specials, streamers, and Woolly Buggers. It's best to carry a supply of these small and large patterns.

The tribe stocks and manages the reservoir and charges a small day-use and camping fee. The reservoir can be fished with all types of gear, but fly fishing usually works best. Sheep Creek Reservoir is in the far northeast quadrant of Nevada. Elko, on Interstate 80 is the closest large city. Take State Route 225 north, 100 miles toward Wild Horse Reservoir and Owyhee, Nevada. Turn west on State Route 11 and go about 12 miles to the reservoir.

Type of Fish
Primarily rainbow trout.

Known Hatches
Damsels, mayflies, and midges.

Equipment to Use
Rods: 4–6 weight 8½'–9'.
Lines: Floating, intermediate, or type II sink to match rod.
Leaders: Sinking line, 6'–7½', 3X–5X. Floating line, 9'–12', 4X–6X.
Reels: Click or disk drag to balance rod.
Wading: Neoprene waders and felt-soled boots are best in winter along most of the shore. Float tubes work well too. Boats can be used only for fishing.

Flies to Use
Dry patterns: Small suspended Midge patterns, Callibaetis Duns, Adult Damsels.
Nymphs: Soft Hackle and small Pheasant Tail (greased and fished just under the surface), Midge Larva or Pupa patterns like Brassies, Black Bird's Nest, Hare's Ear, Damselfly & Dragonfly patterns, Snail, Scud, small Zug Bug & Prince.
Streamers: Sheep Creek Specials! Olive, Brown, and Black Woolly Buggers and Leech patterns. Staynor Ducktail, Black Marabou.

When to Fish
Best in spring and fall before warm water temperatures and weed growth send fish to deeper, cooler depths.

Seasons & Limits
Open year-round, one hour before sunrise to two hours after sunset. Daily limit is five fish for adults (eight in possession) and four for children (six in possession). A tribal fishing permit is required and available from the tribal office in Owyhee, Nevada, the store in Mountain City, or either of the wardens that patrol the area. For more information, contact the Duck Valley Indian Reservation office at (702) 757-3161.

Accommodations & Services
Full services are available 12 miles away in Owyhee. There is unimproved camping at the reservoir with outhouses and water; some spots have tables and cover. Camping is permitted with an overnight permit ($3.00) purchase from the Shoshone-Paiute Tribe.

Rating
Due to higher water temperatures and weed growth during the late summer months, the rating is a 5, then during the spring and fall, this reservoir rates an 8 or 9.

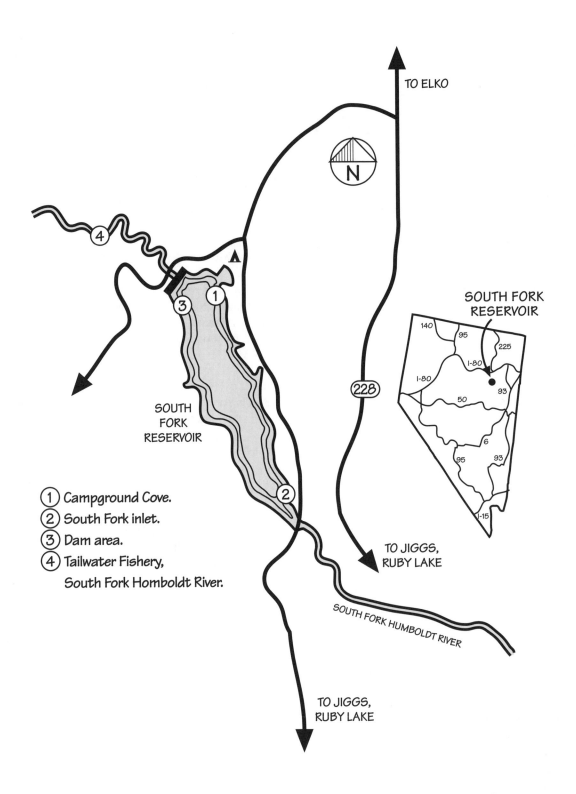

TO ELKO

N

TO JIGGS,
RUBY LAKE

228

SOUTH FORK
RESERVOIR

① Campground Cove.
② South Fork inlet.
③ Dam area.
④ Tailwater Fishery,
   South Fork Homboldt River.

SOUTH FORK HUMBOLDT RIVER

TO JIGGS,
RUBY LAKE

SOUTH FORK
RESERVOIR

140 95 225
I-80 I-80
I-80 50 93
6
95 93
I-15

SOUTH FORK RESERVOIR

NOT TO SCALE

South Fork Reservoir

South Fork Reservoir deserves a spot on every fly angler's "must fish" list of Nevada still waters. As of this writing, it's Nevada's newest trout fishing reservoir. A little history will help with your assessment of this fishery.

The dam on the South Fork of the Humboldt River was completed in 1989. This was right in the middle of a long drought that started in California and Nevada in the mid-1980s. Consequently, it took a while for the reservoir to fill.

While the filling was slow, the fishing was fast and furious. As with any newly created reservoir, freshly flooded land provided a smorgasbord of food for the trout, smallmouth and largemouth bass, and catfish introduced by the Nevada Department of Wildlife.

As with most Nevada still waters, fish South Fork in the spring and fall. You'll avoid the high water temperatures of summer and the water and jet skiers that hatch in great numbers on this popular, multiple-use reservoir as well. Summertime fishermen should try the tailwater fishery below the dam, which has improved dramatically in the last few years.

During the cooler months, watch for trout cruising the shallows, especially along the lower two-thirds of the southern shoreline. Fish for largemouth bass around the willows and other structure at the south end of the reservoir. Concentrate on the rocky face of the dam if you're looking for smallmouth bass.

To get to South Fork Reservoir, take a short 15- to 20-mile drive south of Elko via State Highways 227 and 228. South Fork is a Nevada State Recreation Area, (702) 758-6493.

Type of Fish
Rainbow and brown trout, smallmouth and largemouth bass.

Known Hatches
Damsels, mayflies, and midges.

Equipment to Use
Rods: 4–6 weight 8½'–9'.
Reels: Click or disk drag to balance rod.
Lines: Floating, intermediate, or type II sink line to match rod.
Leaders: Sinking line, 6'–7½', 3X–5X.
Floating line, 9'–12', 4X–6X.
Wading: In hot summer weather, waders are OK. Neoprene waders are a must in winter. A boat or float tube is best here.

Flies to Use
Trout
Dry patterns: Callibaetis Duns, small suspended Midge patterns, Adult Damsels.
Nymphs: Soft Hackles and small Pheasant Tail (greased and fished just under the surface), Midge Larva or Pupa patterns, Brassies, Black Bird's Nest, Hare's Ear, Zug Bug, Prince, Damselfly and Dragonfly patterns, Snails, Scuds.
Streamers: Olive, Brown, or Black Woolly Buggers and Leech patterns, Staynor Ducktails, Sheep Creek Specials, Marabou Streamers, especially in black.

Bass
Assorted poppers and Dahlberg Divers, Woolly Buggers, and Marabou Streamers.

When to Fish
Best in the spring and fall before warm water temperatures send fish to deeper, cooler depths and before the water and jet skier hatch begins in earnest.

Seasons & Limits
Open year-round, any hour of the day or night. Limits of five trout and 15 warmwater fish, of which not more than one can be a black bass with a minimum size of 15". March 1 through June 30 fishing for black bass is catch and release only. The reservoir is usually frozen over during the winter months. Check current regulations.

Accommodations & Services
All services are available 20 miles away in Elko. Limited services nine miles away at Spring Creek Plaza. There is an improved campground at the reservoir with toilets, water, and a boat ramp.

Rating
High water temperatures and multiple-use pressure during the summer months drops this rating to a 5. During the spring and fall, this reservoir can be extremely productive and deserves an 8.

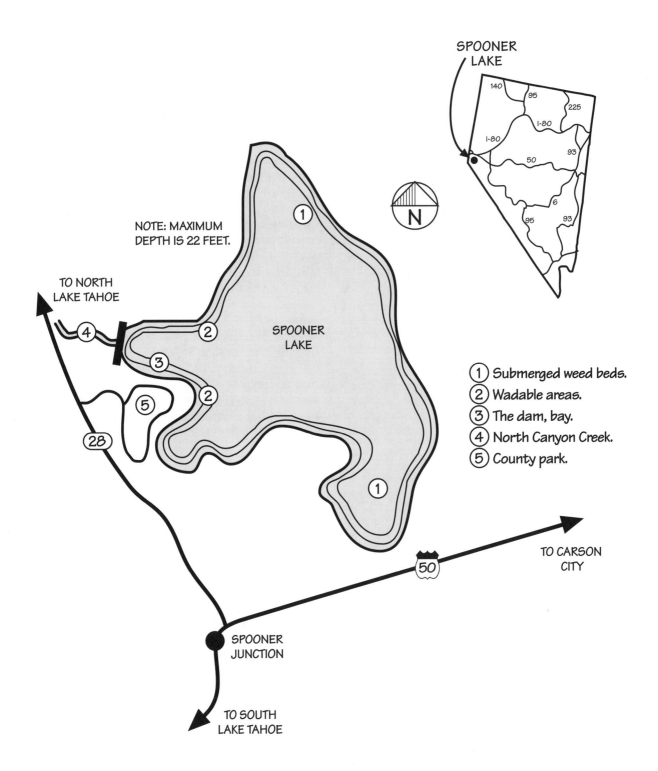

NOTE: MAXIMUM DEPTH IS 22 FEET.

SPOONER LAKE

TO NORTH LAKE TAHOE

TO SOUTH LAKE TAHOE

TO CARSON CITY

SPOONER JUNCTION

(1) Submerged weed beds.
(2) Wadable areas.
(3) The dam, bay.
(4) North Canyon Creek.
(5) County park.

SPOONER LAKE

NOT TO SCALE

Spooner Lake

Located atop Spooner Summit near Lake Tahoe (where Highways 50 and 28 intersect) this 80-acre lake rests in a beautiful mountain meadow. Fed by runoff and small springs, it's one of the few public waters in Nevada with catch and release regulations.

By almost everyone's strict fly fishing standards, Spooner Lake is in the middle of the pack. Adjustments to your standards are warranted if you factor in the high-elevation splendor and great accessibility for beginning fly fishers.

Spooner is most effectively fished from a float tube or small pram. You'll have to carry it (or make the kids haul it) only a couple hundred yards from the convenient parking lot to the water's edge. It's also possible to fly fish from shore, which makes Spooner a popular spot for families with young anglers. Usually by late July, weed beds take over the shoreline. Tubes and prams then become mandatory equipment.

While many lakes and reservoirs suffer the mid-July and August doldrums, Spooner can be alive with consistent hatches. The high elevation of Spooner keeps the water cold late into the season. Midge fishing in the evening can be excellent. Try a tiny Parachute pattern on top of the water with 1'–2' of tippet and a Brassie dangling below. Also, try fishing Damsels, (sinking line) for the brown trout on the bottom.

The rainbows and browns that populate Spooner don't get particularly large. To make up for this the Nevada Department of Wildlife often plants some very large, spawned-out cutthroats. For more information on Spooner Lake contact the Nevada State Recreation Department at (775) 831-0494.

Type of Fish
Primarily rainbow and brown trout. Also the possibility of large cutthroat trout.

Known Hatches & Baitfish
Callibaetis mayflies and damsels, as well as an excellent evening midge hatch. A large population of tui chub provides a lot of trout food. Hatches tend to occur later than those on other Nevada still waters.

Equipment to Use
Rods: 3–6 weight, 8½'–9'.
Reels: Click or disk drag to balance rod.
Line: Floating, intermediate sink, or type II–IV full sink.
Leaders: Sinking 6'–7½', 3X–4X. Floating 9'–12', 5X–7X.
Wading: Neoprene waders to ward off the cold water until late July. In midsummer use a float tube or pram.

Flies to Use
Dry patterns: Suspended Midge patterns, Callibaetis Paranymphs, Parachute Adams, Parachute Hare's Ear, Comparaduns, Adult Damsels.
Nymphs: Damsel, Pheasant Tail, Bird's Nest, Hare's Ear, Soft Hackles, and small Midge Larva or Pupa imitations such as Brassies.

Streamers: Olive, Brown, and Black Woolly Buggers, Leeches. Muddler Minnows, Marabou Muddlers, and Zonkers to imitate the lake's large chub population.

When to Fish
Spooner, because of its high elevation and the fact that it's not fed by a stream, is subject to fish kills during harsh winters. The Nevada Department of Wildlife stocks the lake with trout, which tend to be most eager to bite in June and July.

Seasons & Regulations
Open year-round, but controlled by ice-out and ice-over. Catch and release with single, barbless, artificial lures. Check current regulations.

Accommodations & Services
All services readily available just a few miles west in the many small communities around South Lake Tahoe. A parking fee might be charged at the lake.

Rating
A strict fly fishing rating would put Spooner Lake at a 5.5 or 6. Adjust up to 7 because of the beautiful location and easy access for families and young anglers.

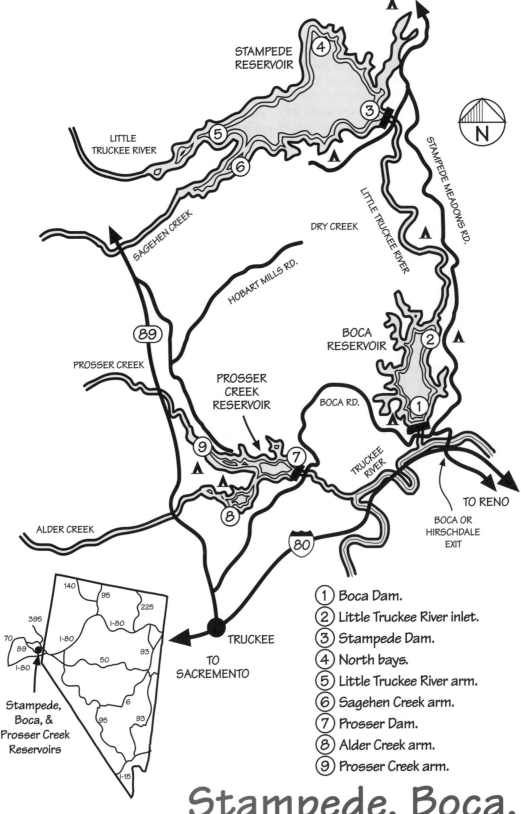

STAMPEDE RESERVOIR

LITTLE TRUCKEE RIVER

STAMPEDE MEADOWS RD.

N

SAGEHEN CREEK

DRY CREEK

LITTLE TRUCKEE RIVER

HOBART MILLS RD.

89

BOCA RESERVOIR

PROSSER CREEK

PROSSER CREEK RESERVOIR

BOCA RD.

TRUCKEE RIVER

TO RENO

BOCA OR HIRSCHDALE EXIT

ALDER CREEK

80

① Boca Dam.
② Little Truckee River inlet.
③ Stampede Dam.
④ North bays.
⑤ Little Truckee River arm.
⑥ Sagehen Creek arm.
⑦ Prosser Dam.
⑧ Alder Creek arm.
⑨ Prosser Creek arm.

TRUCKEE

TO SACREMENTO

Stampede, Boca, & Prosser Creek Reservoirs

140
95
225
395
I-80
70
I-80
89
I-80
50
93
6
95
93
I-15

Stampede, Boca, & Prosser Creek Reservoirs

Stampede, Boca, & Prosser Creek Reservoirs

NOT TO SCALE

Stampede, Boca, & Prosser Creek Reservoirs

These three reservoirs, at 5,800 to 6,000 feet in elevation, were built for water storage on the Truckee River drainage system. They offer a more bite-sized alternative to the nearby giant, Lake Tahoe. Yearly fluctuating water levels, however, can change the fishing conditions. It's not a bad idea to call first for water levels and conditions (Truckee Ranger District (916) 587-3558).

All three reservoirs hold some very large trout and are stocked by the California Department of Fish & Game each year. These waters are readily accessible to the Reno/Tahoe populace, so solitude can be scarce. This fishing is easily accessed from Interstate 80 or off Highway 89 north of Truckee, California.

The inlets of the streams flowing into these impoundments are by far the most productive areas to fly fish, especially early and late in the season. Shallow flats and weed beds provide trout with food and cover and should be stalked and probed. Another productive area at each reservoir is along the base of the dam. This is an especially good spot early in the morning. Big fish cruise these areas looking for baitfish and other prey.

Stampede has a good population of kokanee. These landlocked sockeye salmon offer good sport on a fly rod. In late April and May they can often be found in shallow water (less than 15') and will take a well-presented Blood Midge Larva, small nymph, or Leech pattern. In late September the kokanee in both Boca and Stampede congregate at the feeder stream mouths in preparation for their spawning runs. This is another good opportunity to take them on a fly. Brown trout also ascend these feeder streams at the same time. The largest brown trout I have ever seen in this area was during the fall spawning period. If you are lucky enough to catch one, take a picture and let it go. It has important work to do upstream.

Type of Fish

All three lakes hold healthy populations of rainbow and brown trout. Boca and Stampede contain kokanee salmon. Stampede produces an occasional lake trout.

Known Hatches

Midges, callibaetis, and damselflies.

Equipment to Use

Rods: 5–7 weight, 8½'–9'.
Reels: Click or disk drag.
Line: Floating, intermediate sink, and II and IV full sink lines matched to the rod.
Leaders: Sinking lines, 6'–7½', 3X–4X. Floating lines, 9'–12', 5X–7X.
Wading: All reservoirs have many areas to wade. Float tubing is popular, though 3,400-acre Stampede is a bit intimidating. Boats are helpful.

Flies to Use

Dry patterns: Midge patterns (particularly the Blood Midge), Callibaetis, Elk Hair Caddis, Parachute Adams, Parachute Hare's Ears, Adult Damsels.
Nymphs: Damsels, Pheasant Tail, Zug Bug, Hare's Ear, Sheep Creek Special, Black Bird's Nest, Blood Midge Larva.
Streamers: Various big streamers, Woolly Buggers, and Leeches.

When to Fish

The best times are from ice-out to late June, then from mid-September to the winter freeze.

Seasons & Limits

Open all year with general limits. Consult the *California Sport Fishing Regulations* or visit a local fly shop for more details.

Accommodations & Services

Everything one needs is approximately 20 miles away in downtown Reno or 10 miles away in Truckee, California. There are improved Forest Service campgrounds at all three reservoirs and a full-service RV park and general store at the United Trails Campground. Take the Boca exit off Interstate 80 for these services.

Rating

Early in the season Prosser and Boca can be a strong 7 or an 8 for the fly fisher. Boca, with all the wind surfers and jet skiers, rates barely a 5 during summer months. Stampede, just after ice-out, then in late spring and again in late September and October earns a solid 8.

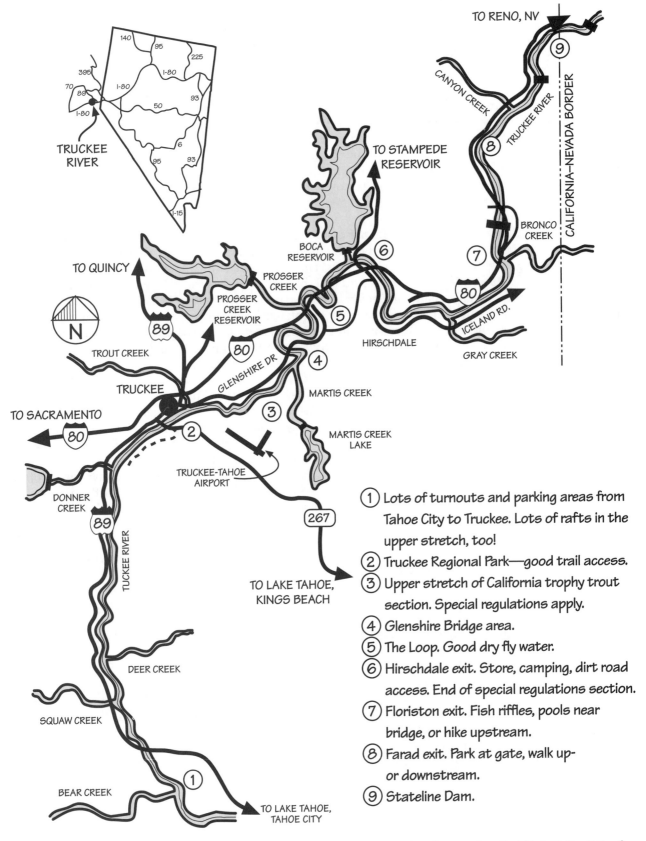

1. Lots of turnouts and parking areas from Tahoe City to Truckee. Lots of rafts in the upper stretch, too!
2. Truckee Regional Park—good trail access.
3. Upper stretch of California trophy trout section. Special regulations apply.
4. Glenshire Bridge area.
5. The Loop. Good dry fly water.
6. Hirschdale exit. Store, camping, dirt road access. End of special regulations section.
7. Floriston exit. Fish riffles, pools near bridge, or hike upstream.
8. Farad exit. Park at gate, walk up- or downstream.
9. Stateline Dam.

TRUCKEE RIVER, CALIFORNIA

NOT TO SCALE

Truckee River

The Truckee, the largest of the three major rivers in the Reno area, provides year-round fly fishing. Easy access, beautiful canyon scenery, and fiesty wild trout earn the Truckee an easy 8 on the quality-of-fly-fishing scale. The truth is, overall, the Truckee is a tough river to fly fish.

Wide and fast in some areas, this freestone stream can be very tricky to wade. Proper presentations are difficult to make in the pocket water, big riffles, and deep runs. Success here requires skill in getting the right flies in front of the fish. When nymphing, use long leaders of 9 feet or more and a split shot and indicator setup to reach the bottom. Bring lots of flies and be prepared to match prevailing hatches. Try streamers in the spring and fall in the deeper runs and pools. Use them elsewhere all year.

The Truckee drains huge Lake Tahoe, flowing north and east from the lake through the town of Truckee, California, where the better fishing begins. It then tumbles through a steep, forested canyon down the eastern slope of the Sierra Nevada and through the city of Reno. From Reno it flows 35 miles to the north, into the desert and into one of the state's famous fisheries, Pyramid Lake.

Access to the Truckee is great. From the town of Truckee to the state border, the canyon stretch of the river is accessed off Interstate 80. One's fly fishing is reasonably unaffected despite proximity to a major, all-weather freeway. The best fly fishing water is between Truckee and the town of Verdi, Nevada, a small community west of Reno.

When the river enters Nevada, it slows down and provides more opportunity to fish flat water. However in the late summer months the water temperature rises and the best fishing is in the cooler canyon area upstream. Tributaries to the Truckee are also productive, particularly the Little Truckee River. Here there are excellent hatches and large populations of trout as well.

Types of Fish

Rainbow and brown trout with isolated populations of cutthroat and brookies. Average fish are 10"–12", but trout of 18" plus are not uncommon. A fish over 20" would be considered a trophy. Whitefish also populate the Truckee and can provide good sport, especially during winter months.

Known Hatches

A variety of caddisflies hatch regularly on the river from late May through October. Green rock worm is the most prevalant caddis. Golden stone and little yellow stone nymphs are found most everywhere. Sporadic mayfly hatches also occur throughout the warmer months including a fair-to-good green drake hatch in early June. The most reliable hatch for summer dry fly fishing is the little yellow stone. It comes off from mid-June into late August and early September. Midge hatches are consistent throughout the year, including winter, when fishing during warm spells is highly recommended.

Equipment to Use

Rods: 5–6 weight, 9'.
Reels: Mechanical or palm drag.
Line: Floating. Sink tip for deep holes or runs.
Leaders: 9'–10', 4X–6X.
Wading: The Truckee is a difficult stream to wade. Felt-soled boots are a must. A wading staff is recommended.

Flies to Use

Dry patterns: Adams, Humpy, Royal Wulff, Stimulators, Elk Hair Caddis, Parachute Hare's Ear and other Parachute patterns in various colors, Little Yellow Stone patterns, Ants, and Hoppers.
Nymphs: Bird's Nest, Gold Ribbed Hare's Ear, Prince, Zug Bug, and any of these with a beadhead. Also use a variety of Soft Hackles and Caddis Larva Emergers, as well as the Western Coachman.
Streamers: Muddler Minnow, Woolly Bugger, Zonker, and Matuka. Sculpins are common in the Truckee.

When to Fish

Very reliable evening and some morning dry fly action from late May to mid-October. Nymphs are productive year-round.

Seasons & Limits

California: Last Saturday in April to November 15.
Nevada: Open all year.
There are a variety of special regulations on both the California and Nevada sections of the Truckee; make sure you check the appropriate regulations!

Accommodations & Services

All services are readily available in the Reno, Tahoe, and Truckee areas.

Rating

During the summer months the Truckee rates an 8. Year-round nymph fishing also deserves an 8.

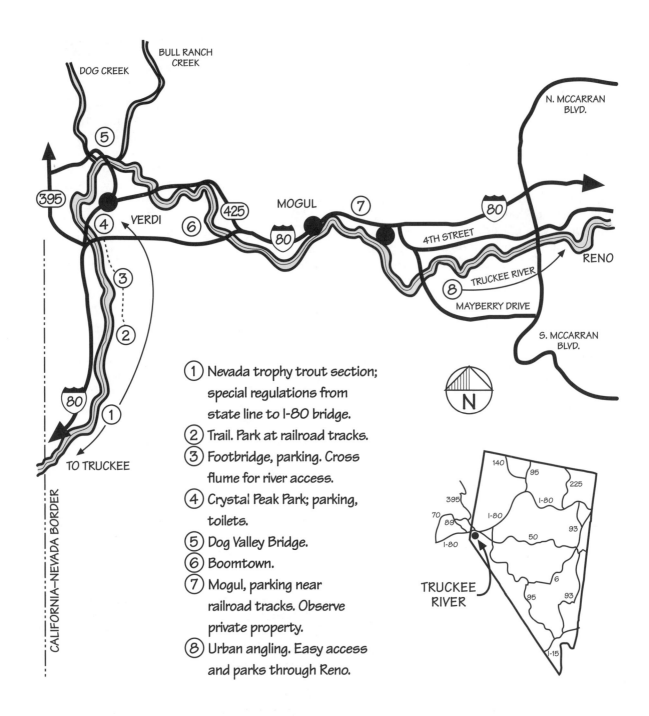

1. Nevada trophy trout section; special regulations from state line to I-80 bridge.
2. Trail. Park at railroad tracks.
3. Footbridge, parking. Cross flume for river access.
4. Crystal Peak Park; parking, toilets.
5. Dog Valley Bridge.
6. Boomtown.
7. Mogul, parking near railroad tracks. Observe private property.
8. Urban angling. Easy access and parks through Reno.

TRUCKEE RIVER, NEVADA

NOT TO SCALE

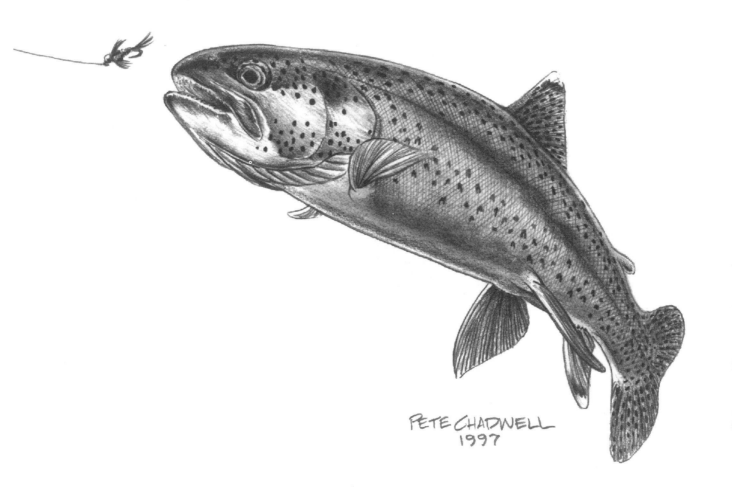

Rainbow Trout

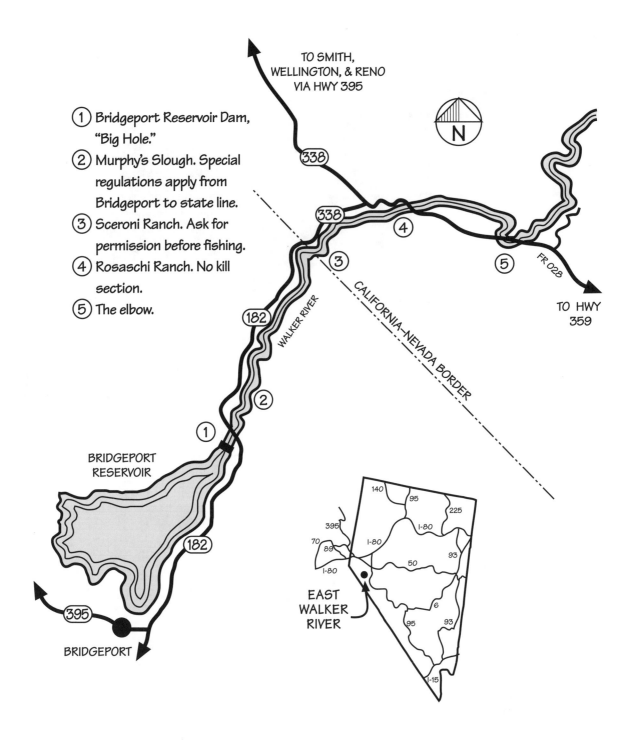

① Bridgeport Reservoir Dam, "Big Hole."
② Murphy's Slough. Special regulations apply from Bridgeport to state line.
③ Sceroni Ranch. Ask for permission before fishing.
④ Rosaschi Ranch. No kill section.
⑤ The elbow.

WALKER RIVER, EAST FORK

NOT TO SCALE

Walker River
East Fork

The East Fork of the Walker River, below Bridgeport Reservoir, has long been a popular destination for the avid fly angler. In years past, the fast riffles and deep, powerful runs of this section were rated, in terms of fish per mile, one of California's top trout streams.

Easily accessible as it flows alongside Highway 182 (from Bridgeport, California, to the Nevada state line) this section offers serious nymph and streamer anglers opportunities to catch trophy rainbow or brown trout, especially if you avoid the weekend crowds. Twenty-inch fish are common in this stretch of the river. In the spring or fall, stripping a Woolly Bugger or Zonker tempts any rod-bender within chomping distance.

The famed "Big Hole," where Bridgeport Reservoir waters pour into a basin prior to entering the stream channel, and the stretch below it are, for the fly fisher, some of the most difficult and potentially rewarding spots on the river.

In Nevada, the East Walker flows through sagebrush flats and is known for consistent insect hatches and large fish. That's why it's considered by many the best trout stream in the state. Summer irrigation demands, however, can make water levels fluctuate. While some of the river courses through private land, public access is readily available on the significant portion of the river that runs through land controlled by the Bureau of Land Management and the U.S. Forest Service. The summer snake season also bears mention: Be careful.

Open year-round, the Nevada section of the East Walker offers the winter fly fisher excellent stream angling. Large populations of stoneflies provide exceptional year-round nymph fishing. If you like to fish streamers, large browns and rainbows are taken using big flies and sink tip lines.

Type of Fish
Rainbow and brown trout and mountain whitefish.

Known Hatches
Golden stoneflies hatch prior to or just at the beginning of runoff, usually in March or April. Mayflies also begin to appear in March, coming off sporadically throughout the warmer months and into late September and early October. Like on the Truckee and Carson rivers, caddis are the most prolific insect in the Walker drainage: Huge hatches occur in the summer. Also in summer look for little yellow stones. Baitfish to consider are sculpin, chubs, dace, and trout fry.

Equipment to Use
Rods: 5–6 weight, 9'.
Reels: Palm or disk drag.
Line: Floating, use sink tips for deep holes or runs.
Leaders: 7½'–10', 3X–6X.
Wading: Moderately difficult. Wear felt-soled boots and use a wading staff in the gnarlier sections.

Flies to Use
Dry patterns: Adams, Humpy, Royal Wulff, Blue-Winged Olive, Elk Hair Caddis, Parachute Hare's Ear, other Parachute patterns in various colors, Little Yellow Stone patterns, Ants, and Hoppers.
Nymphs: Bird's Nest, Gold Ribbed Hare's Ear, Prince, Zug Bug, any of these with beadheads. Green Rock Worm patterns to imitate the prevalent caddis, Golden Stone and Little Yellow Stone, various Soft Hackles and Caddis Larva, Pupa, and Emergers, Western Coachman.
Streamers: Muddler Minnow, Woolly Bugger, Hornberg, Zonker, and Matuka.

When to Fish
March, when the water is low and the stonefly hatch is on, is the best fly fishing. June–July, when caddis are hatching, and September–October are good for Hopper dry fly action. Nymphs and streamers are productive year-round. On the East Walker in Nevada, late fall through March can be outstanding when low, clear water conditions prevail.

Seasons & Limits
California: Last Saturday in April to November 15.
Nevada: Open all year.
Special regulations apply on the California and Nevada sections. Check state regulations.

Accommodations & Services
All services in larger towns like Gardnerville, Nevada, and Bridgeport, California. Limited services in Wellington, Nevada, and at Topaz Lake.

Rating
Productive dry and nymph fishing and outstanding streamer action for large trout, a solid 9.

59

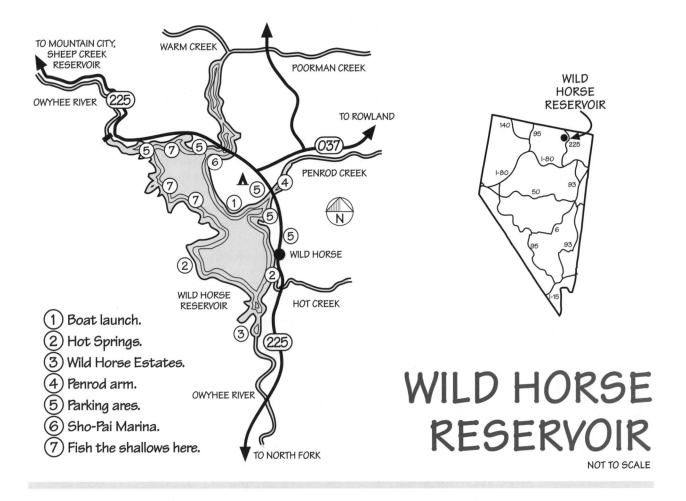

TO MOUNTAIN CITY, SHEEP CREEK RESERVOIR

WARM CREEK

POORMAN CREEK

TO ROWLAND

OWYHEE RIVER (225)

(037)

PENROD CREEK

N

WILD HORSE

HOT CREEK

WILD HORSE RESERVOIR

(225)

OWYHEE RIVER

TO NORTH FORK

① Boat launch.
② Hot Springs.
③ Wild Horse Estates.
④ Penrod arm.
⑤ Parking ares.
⑥ Sho-Pai Marina.
⑦ Fish the shallows here.

WILD
HORSE
RESERVOIR

140 95
I-80 225
I-80
50 93
6
95 93
I-15

WILD HORSE RESERVOIR

NOT TO SCALE

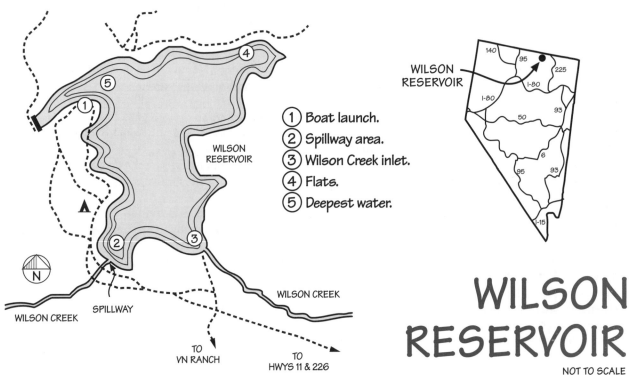

WILSON RESERVOIR

N

WILSON CREEK

SPILLWAY

WILSON CREEK

TO VN RANCH

TO HWYS 11 & 226

WILSON CREEK

① Boat launch.
② Spillway area.
③ Wilson Creek inlet.
④ Flats.
⑤ Deepest water.

WILSON RESERVOIR

140 95
I-80 225
I-80
50 93
6
95 93
I-15

WILSON RESERVOIR

NOT TO SCALE

Wild Horse & Wilson Reservoirs

Due to their proximity and method of fishing, Wild Horse and Wilson reservoirs are presented together on these pages.

Wild Horse Reservoir has long been a favorite of anglers who have learned to appreciate fly fishing high desert still waters. Once you're in the far north central part of Nevada, the fishing is easy to get to. The reservoir parallels State Highway 225, approximately 65 miles north of Elko.

Wild Horse was created in 1937 when the original dam was constructed on the East Fork of the Owyhee River. The dam was rebuilt in 1970. At maximum pool, 2,800 surface acres of water are impounded and the reservoir runs 60 to 70 feet deep near the dam. Wild Horse is a Nevada State Recreation Area (702) 758-6493.

There are populations of bass, crappie, and catfish in Wild Horse. The Nevada Department of Wildlife, however, manages the water primarily as a quality trout fishery. Thousands of 8" to 10" rainbows are planted in the spring and fall. Due to the rich food supply in the reservoir, these fish waste little time reaching an average size of around 18", with many trout reaching trophy proportions.

Wilson Reservoir was constructed in 1954 as an irrigation water impoundment. At 800 surface acres and 30 feet deep, it's a smaller cousin to Wild Horse. Much like Wild Horse, Wilson fly fishes best in the spring and fall. Fish from shore or from a float tube or boat, casting along drop-offs and to fish working in the shallows.

Bass fishing is best in late spring and summer and provides good angling opportunities even for inexperienced fly fishers. Poppers can produce on the surface while large Leech, Streamer, and Woolly Bugger patterns are good subsurface choices. Anglers fishing these reservoirs should concentrate on the inlet stream areas and shallows with large weed beds. For a change of pace, give the outflow streams below the dams a try.

Although Wilson is almost directly west of Wild Horse (as the crow flies), you have to take State Highway 225 north out of Elko to Highway 226 northwest to Tuscarora to reach the reservoir.

Type of Fish
Primarily rainbow and brown trout, and largemouth bass, crappie, and catfish.

Known Hatches
Damsels, mayflies, and midges.

Equipment to Use
Rods: 4–6 weight, 8½'–9'.
Reels: Click or disk drag.
Lines: Floating, intermediate, or II sink lines to match rod.
Leaders: Sinking line, 6'–7½', 3X–5X. Floating line, 9'–12', 4X–6X.
Wading: From shore, hippers OK. Best to use a boat or float tube.

Flies to Use
Dry patterns: Adult damsels, small suspended Midges, Callibaetis Duns.
Nymphs: Damselfly and Dragonfly patterns. Soft Hackles, small Pheasant Tail (greased, fished just under the surface). Midge Larva and Pupa patterns, Brassies, Black Bird's Nest, Hare's Ear, Zug Bug, Prince, Snail, Scuds.
Streamers: Marabous, especially in black. Olive, Brown, and Black Woolly Buggers, and Leech patterns, Staynor Ducktail, Sheep Creek Special.

When to Fish
Fly fishing is best in the spring and fall. In the summer, warmwater sends fish deep into the cooler, out-of-reach areas.

Seasons & Limits
Wild Horse: Open year-round, all day. Limit five trout and 15 warmwater game fish of which not more than five may be black bass no smaller than 11". March 1 through June 30, black bass fishing is catch and release only.
Wilson Sink: Same as Wild Horse except the black bass limit is 10, minimum size 11". Check Current regulations. Both reservoirs freeze over during winter.

Accommodations & Services
Wild Horse: All services in Elko or Owyhee, Nevada. Several campgrounds around the reservoir range from full-service to primitive. Wild Horse State Park has camping, day-use, and boat launch facilities. Launch at Sho-Pai campground. Wild Horse Resort Motel has an RV park, restaurant, and convenience store.
Wilson Sink: BLM campground and boat launch with water, restrooms, and trailer dump. Closest lodging, food, and gas are in the town of Tuscarora, Nevada.

Rating
Late summer ratings drop to a 5. In late spring, early summer, and fall, fly fishing the shallow coves and bays of both reservoirs can be extremely productive and rate an 8. Bass fishing in Wilson rates an 8.

Other Nevada Rivers, Creeks, & Streams

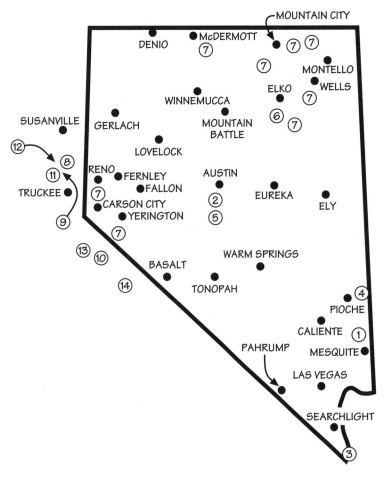

Nevada Creeks (see p. 63)

1. Beaver Dam Wash
2. Big Creek
3. Colorado River
4. Eagle Valley Creek
5. Kingston Creek
6. Humboldt River, South Fork
7. Northern and Western

Northeastern Sierra (see p. 63)

8. Last Chance Creek
9. Little Truckee River
10. Pleasant Valley Creek
11. Prosser Creek
12. Sagehen Creek
13. Carson River, West Fork
14. Walker River, West Fork

Type of Fish

Rainbow, brown, brook, and cutthroat trout.

Known Hatches

Caddis found in all waters. Look for mayflies and terrestrials, depending on the season and conditions.

Equipment to Use

Rods: 3–5 weight, 7'–9'.
Reels: Mechanical or palm drag is fine.
Line: Floating. Carry sink tip for occasional use.
Leaders: Short! 7½' is usually plenty.
Wading: Easy to difficult depending on water levels. Felt-soled boots help. Waders when the water is high and cold. In warm weather, wet-wading is OK.

Flies to Use

Dries: Royal Wulff, Humpy, Adams, Parachute Hare's Ear, Elk Hair Caddis, Foam Ant, hoppers.
Nymphs: Prince, Bird's Nest, Hare's Ear, Zug Bug, Pheasant Tail.
Streamers: Zonker, Muddler, Woolly Bugger.

When to Fish

After spring runoff through the fall.

Seasons & Limits

Variable. Consult fly shops and California and Nevada fishing seasons and regulations.

Accommodations and Services

Variable, ranging from none to some. Check local fly shops.

Rating

If you try these waters at a good time of year, the fishing is an 8. Simplicity, no crowds, and the overall experience of fishing these small waters makes them almost always a 10.

Other Rivers, Streams, & Creeks
Comments on Lesser-Known
Nevada and Northeastern Sierra Fly Fishing Waters

Our region has many small and lesser-known fly fishing opportunities we categorize as "other." They offer fair to possibly good fly fishing depending on water quality and temperatures. Investigating these smaller desert and alpine waters provides you with uncrowded fishing, beautiful scenery, and challenging angling experiences.

In general, and in good water years, fish after runoff through the fall. Drastic fluctuations in water levels due to that year's snowpack, can occur in several of these drainages. Treat these places with the respect you accord major waters. As always, check at a fly shop or ask a local for more information.

Nevada

1. Beaver Dam Wash—Located in Beaver Dam State Park in eastern Lincoln County, this water provides stream fishing for rainbow trout above and below Schroeder Reservoir (see "Other Still Waters").

2. Big Creek—Approximately 10 miles south of Austin, Big Creek runs through the Reese River Valley and offers excellent small stream and beaver pond angling for rainbow and brown trout.

3. Colorado River—The quality of this year-round fishery for striped and largemouth bass and rainbow trout (below Davis Dam at Laughlin) depends greatly on water releases from the dam and the seasonal movements of the striped bass.

4. Eagle Valley Creek—Flowing in and out of Eagle Valley Reservoir, this creek offers fly fishing for rainbow and brown trout. It's located about 16 miles east of Pioche off State Route 322 (see Eagle Valley Reservoir in "Other Still Waters").

5. Kingston Creek—Flowing through Kingston Canyon in the Humboldt–Toiyabe National Forest, Kingston Creek provides the water for Groves Lake (see "Other Still Waters"). You'll find some excellent small stream fishing for rainbows, browns, and brookies.

6. Humboldt River, South Fork—Above and below the new South Fork Reservoir, this water is providing some of the best stream fishing in the northeastern part of the state. Species are as varied as rainbow, hybrid rainbow, brown, cutthroat, and brook trout, mountain whitefish, and even smallmouth bass. If you stray out of the state park, be sure to respect private lands.

7. Northern and Western Nevada Creeks— From the eastern Sierra to the Utah border a number of small streams have populations of wild and stocked trout. In good water years all offer very good fly fishing from right after runoff through the fall. Literally hundreds of small high desert and alpine streams and creeks are found in remote areas such as the Santa Rosa, Independence, Jarbidge, Ruby, and East Humboldt mountain ranges and the O'Neil Basin. These waters contain fish and offer the adventurous four-wheel-driving or backpacking angler the threefold reward of solitude, gorgeous desert and alpine vistas, and great fly fishing, mostly for relatively small but eager rainbow, brown, and cutthroat trout.

Northeastern Sierra

8. Last Chance Creek—Just 40 miles north of Reno, this small freestone stream is created by the outflow of Frenchman Lake. It is fished heavily by all types but still offers fly anglers a good spot to stream-fish close to town and early in the season.

9. Little Truckee River—Flowing from headwaters at Webber Lake (private) to its confluence with the main Truckee River, this small but beautiful stream can be extremely rewarding for the angler fishing for rainbow and brown trout and spawning kokanee (in the fall). Early- or late-season anglers can fish to large trout where this stream flows into Stampede and Boca reservoirs. Excellent summer hatches make this a good choice for the dry fly enthusiast.

10. Pleasant Valley Creek—A very small but productive stream flowing just outside Markleeville, this gently meandering water is used heavily. But due to special regulations it still offers excellent fly fishing for rainbows and an occasional cutthroat.

11. Prosser Creek—Above and below Prosser Creek Reservoir, this small, freestone stream offers good nymph and dry fly action. Anglers must walk a little. In the spring, spawning rainbows from the Truckee River are found in the stretch below the dam.

12. Sagehen Creek—A smaller version of the Little Truckee River, this creek has rainbow, brown, and brook trout and a fall run of spawning kokanee from Stampede Reservoir. An excellent place to fish if you want to avoid the crowds on other, more popular waters.

13. Carson River, West Fork—Running just south of South Lake Tahoe and alongside Highway 88, this small stream offers a variety of water: from the spring creek-type water of Hope Valley and Picket Meadows to plunge-pool, pocket water by Sorensen's Resort toward Woodfords. Stocked by California Fish & Game with catchable rainbows and browns, this is an excellent place to introduce a novice to stream fly fishing.

14. Walker River, West Fork—The flood of '97 greatly changed this easy-access, popular stretch of water along Highway 395. It flows through the river canyon above Topaz Lake. Upstream in Pickle Meadow, anglers can still enjoy good fishing in a beautiful alpine setting. Below Topaz Lake in Nevada, most of the river runs through private land and access is limited.

Other Nevada Still Waters

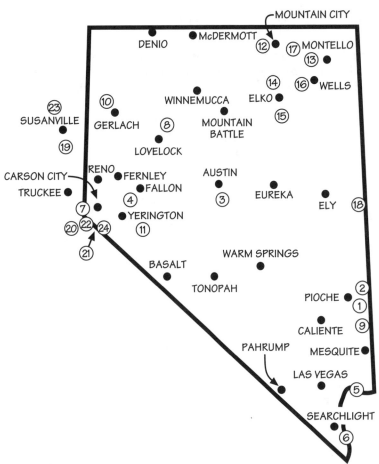

Nevada (see p. 65)
1. Echo Canyon Reservoir
2. Eagle Valley Reservoir
3. Groves Lake
4. Lahontan Reservoir
5. Lake Mead
6. Lake Mohave
7. Lake Tahoe
8. Rye patch Reservoir
9. Schroeder Reservoir
10. Squaw Creek Reservoir
11. Walker Lake
12. Dry Creek Reservoir
13. Jakes Creek Reservoir
14. Dorsey Reservoir
15. Jiggs/Zunino Reservoir
16. Angel Lakes
17. Emerald Lake
18. Baker and Johnson Lakes

Northeastern Sierra (see p. 65)
19. Antelope lake
20. Blue and Caples Lakes
21. Heenan Lake
22. Indian Creek Reservoir
23. McCoy Flat Reservoir
24. Topaz Lake

Type of Fish
Rainbow, brown, brook, and cutthroat trout, bass, panfish.

Known Hatches
Mayflies, damselflies, and midges.

Equipment to Use
Rods: 4–7 weight.
Line: Floating, full sink intermediate to IVs.
Leaders: 6'–9', 4X–7X.
Reels: Standard trout reels are fine.
Wading: Most of these waters have wadable shorelines. Best to take a float tube or small pram.

Flies to Use
Dries: Suspended Midge, Parachute in light and dark colors. Small Royal Wulff, Elk Hair Caddis, Adult Damsel.
Nymphs: Scud, Damsel, Dragonfly, Midge, Snail, Sheep Creek Special, Gold Ribbed Hare's Ear, Pheasant Tail, Bird's Nest.
Streamers: Woolly Buggers, Leech patterns.

When to Fish
Ice-out to ice-up. Walker Lake does not freeze over.

Seasons and Limits
Complex and varied with the water. Check regulations.

Accommodations and Services
Some, variable, or none! Camp or ask around.

Rating
When conditions are good, all are 8 or better.

Other Still Waters
Comments on Other Nevada
and Northeastern Sierra Fly Fishing Waters

This region has a lot of still water that isn't well known and is often a great alternative to overcrowded waters. As a group these "others" offer some reliable fly fishing. Droughts and irrigation can severely affect many of Nevada's smaller waters. Get up-to-date conditions from the resources in the back of this guidebook and area fly shops.

Nevada

1. Echo Canyon Reservoir—These 70 acres, located 12 miles east of Pioche in the Echo Canyon State Park, contain stocked rainbow trout, largemouth bass, and white crappie.

2. Eagle Valley Reservoir—Good fishing for stocked rainbow and brown trout on these 61 acres. Fish in the spring and fall when water temperatures are more hospitable to the fish (see Eagle Valley Creek in "Other Rivers, Streams, & Creeks").

3. Groves Lake—Populated by rainbow, brown, and brook trout. Best fly fished in spring to early summer and in the fall. Located 30 miles south of Austin, Nevada, off State Route 376.

4. Lahontan Reservoir—In the Lahontan State Recreation Area (20 miles west of Fallon, Nevada, off Highway 50), this large multiuse impoundment offers fly angling for trout, largemouth bass, white bass, wipers, and walleye. Fish in late spring after the water clears and before it heats up. A multitude of boats and jet skis accompany the summer sun here. State Recreation Area (702) 577-2226.

5. Lake Mead—The largest reservoir in North America. During spring and fall, float tube fly fishing for striped bass is popular. In winter, rainbows are stocked in the Boulder Basin area, near Las Vegas.

6. Lake Mohave—A year-round fishery for striped and largemouth bass and channel catfish. Rainbows are stocked all year in the cooler water above Eldorado Canyon. They're stocked during the winter months off the Nevada shoreline in the lower lake.

7. Lake Tahoe—Depths of up to 1,600 feet make this a favorite for trollers and deep-liners looking for lake and rainbow trout and naturally spawning kokanee salmon. Fly fishers can cast to rainbows in the shallows around Cave Rock and Sand Harbor. Tahoe is a year-round mecca for tourists and outdoor enthusiasts. State Recreation Area (702) 831-0494.

8. Rye Patch Reservoir—At 10,800 surface acres, this is the largest impoundment in northwestern Nevada. It supports warmwater white crappie, walleye, channel catfish, and largemouth and spotted bass. In the spring during good water years, fly fish the outflow below the dam for walleye. Sometimes after low water the Nevada Department of Wildlife stocks trout. The state park has a boat launch and campground. Go 25 miles north of Lovelock, Nevada just off Interstate 80. State Recreation Area (702) 538-7321.

9. Schroeder Reservoir— Rainbow trout are stocked annually on this put-and-take, 14-acre reservoir (see Beaver Dam Wash in "Other Rivers, Streams, & Creeks").

10. Squaw Creek Reservoir— Fished heavily during warm months, this is the one of the first waters to ice-out in the early spring. Then it offers some excellent and uncrowded Midge and Streamer fishing for various stocked trout, brown bullhead, and largemouth bass. Go 15 miles north of Gerlach, Nevada, and look for an RV campground off Highway 447.

11. Walker Lake—From November to May, this large desert lake (north of Hawthorne on Highway 95) can offer excellent fly fishing for cutthroat trout. Use intermediate or type II lines and a variety of light and dark Woolly Worms.

12–15. Other trout reservoirs: Dry Creek, west of Mountain City; **Jakes Creek**, off Highway 93 north of Wells; **Dorsey**, near Elko; **Jiggs or Zunino**, south of Elko past South Fork on Highway 228.

16–18. Other trout lakes: Angel, south of Wells; a series of 14 lakes in the Ruby Mountains; **Emerald**, in the Jarbidge Mountains, **Baker and Johnson Lakes** (in Great Basin National Park) for backpackers seeking alpine scenery and excellent trout fishing. Several private waters are available on a fee basis and are listed elsewhere in this guide.

Northeastern Sierra

19. Antelope Lake—A warm- and coldwater fishery. Easy access campgrounds by the lake and good fishing from shore, boats, or float tubes make this a popular family spot.

20. Blue and Caples Lakes—Typical mid-altitude Sierra lakes. Cold water temperatures throughout the summer season provide fly fishers reliable fishing into August. The fish make up for their small size with large numbers.

21. Heenan Lake—Located off Highway 89 southeast of Markleeville, California's cutthroat broodstock lake is open from the Friday before Labor Day to October 31, Friday to Sunday only. Fly anglers have the chance to catch a cutthroat of a lifetime here.

22. Indian Creek Reservoir— Usually accessible by late February or March, it provides good early-season angling that often continues through June.

23. McCoy Flat Reservoir—Excellent when not drained by irrigators. McCoy's biomass produces huge trout in a short period of time.

24. Topaz Lake—On the Nevada/California border, 1,200-acre Topaz opens January 1. Midge and Streamer angling here help shake the winter "blahs." Much of the lake is deep and hard to fly fish, but the shallow south end (where the West Walker enters) is usually productive. Wade the rocky west shoreline or fish it from a boat or float tube.

Appendix

Nevada & Northeastern Sierra Fly Fishing Resources

Nevada

Anglers Edge
(775) 782-4734
1589 US Highway 395 S.
Gardnerville, NV 89410

The Gilly Fishing Store
(775) 358-6113
1111 Rock Blvd.
Sparks, NV 89431

Las Vegas Fly Fishing
Shawn Saunders
7520 Washington Ave.
Suite 140
Las Vegas, NV 89128
(702) 838-6669
www.lvflyfish.com

Mark Fore & Strike
   Sporting Goods Store
Marty Piccinini
490 Kietzke Lane
Reno, NV 89502
(775) 322-9559

Pyramid Lake Store
George & Carla Molino
29555 Pyramid Lake Road
Reno, NV 89510
(775) 476-0555
www.fishpyramid.com

Reno Fly Shop
Dave Stanley
294 E. Moana Lane #14
Reno, NV 89502
(775) 825-3474
www.renoflyshop.com

Tahoe Area

Alpine Fly Fishing
Jim Crouse
P.O. Box 10465
South Lake Tahoe, CA
   96158

Four Seasons Fly Fishing
P.O. Box 5122
Tahoe City, CA 96145
(530) 550-9780
www.flyfishingtruckee-
tahoe.com

Mountain Hardware
   & Sports
Tom Brochu
11320 Donner Pass Rd.
Truckee, CA 96161
(530) 587-4844

Ralph & Lisa Cutter's
   California School
   of Fly Fishing
Ralph & Lisa Cutter
P.O. Box 8212
Truckee, CA 96162
(530) 587-7005
(800) 588-7688

Stillwaters Guide Service
Chris Wharton
5410 Simmons Drive
Reno, NV 89523
(775) 747-0312
www.out4trout.com

Tahoe Fly Fishing
   Outfitters
Victor Bennet
2705 Lake Tahoe Blvd.
South Lake Tahoe, CA
   96150
(530) 541-8208
www.tahoeflyfishing.com

Truckee River Outfitters
Dave Stanley
10200 Donner Pass Rd.
Truckee, CA 96161
(530) 582-0900
   (Late April—September)
(775) 825-3474
   (October–Early April)
www.renoflyshop.com

San Francisco Area

Leland Fly Fishing
   Outfitters
Joe Frazier
463 Bush Street
San Francisco, CA 94108
(415) 781-3474
www.flyfishingoutfitters.
com

Orvis San Francisco
248 Sutter Street
San Francisco, CA 94108
(415) 392-1600
www.orvis.com

Northern California

Brock's Fly Fishing
   Specialist
Gary Gunsolley
100 N. Main Street
Bishop, CA 93514
(760) 872-3581
www.brocksflyfish.com

Fly Fishing Specialties
Stan Hellikson
6412-C Tupelo Drive
Citrus Heights, CA 95621
(916) 722-1055
www.flyfishingspecialties.
com

The Fly Shop
Michael Michalak
4140 Churn Creek Road
Redding, CA 96002
(800) 669-3474
www.theflyshop.com

Gold Rush Sporting Goods
Tammy Milby
196 East Sierra Street
Portola, CA 96122
(530) 832-5724

Grizzly Country Store
Lake Davis Road
Portola, CA 96122
(530) 832-0270

Kiene's Fly Shop
Bill & Marilyn Kiene
2654 Marconi Ave.
Sacramento, CA 95821
(916) 486-9958
www.kiene.com

Sportsman's Den
Allen Bruzza
1580 East Main Street
Quincy, CA 95971
(530) 283-2733

California Foothills

Mother Lode Fly Shop
14841 Mono Way
E. Sonora, CA 95327
(209) 532-8600

Nevada City Anglers
Tony Dumont
417 Broad St.
Nevada City, CA 95959
(530) 478-9301
www.nevadacityanglers.
com

White Pines Outdoors
Dan Liechty
2182 Highway 4
Arnold, CA 95223
(209) 795-1054

Southern California

Bell's Sporting
    Goods & Hardware
Highway 395
Lee Vining, CA 93541
(760) 647-6406

Buz Buzek's Fly Shop
Buz Buzek
110 West Main Street
Suite D
Visalia, CA 93291
(559) 734-1151

Ken's Alpine Shop &
    Sporting Goods
258 Main Street
Bridgeport, CA 93517
(760) 932-7707

Trout Fitters
Kent Rianda
Shellmart Center #4–5
Mammoth Lakes, CA 93517
(760) 924-3676
www.thetroutfitter.com

The Trout Fly
Highway 20 &
    Mammoth Rd.
Gateway Center
Mammoth Lakes, CA
    93546
(760) 934-2417
www.thetroutfly.com

Village Sport Shop
Yosemite Village
Yosemite Park, CA 95389
(209) 372-1286

Yosemite Angler
49er Shopping Center
Mariposa, CA 95350
(209) 966-8377

Clubs & Associations

California Trout
870 Market Street
Suite 528
San Francisco, CA 94102
(415) 392-8887
www.caltrout.org

Federation of Fly Fishers
National Headquarters
P.O. Box 1595
Bozeman, MT 59771
(460) 585-7592
www.fedflyfishers.org

Great Basin Bassers
*Call The Gilly Fishing Store
    for current contact
    number.*

International Game & Fish
    Association
300 Gulf Stream Way
Dania Beach, FL 33004
(954) 927-2628
www.igfa.org

Las Vegas Fly Fishing Club
4747 Vegas Drive
Las Vegas, NV 89117
http://members.aol.com/
    flyfyshkid/flyfishing.htm

National Fresh Water
    Fishing Hall of Fame
P.O. Box 690
Hayward, WI 54843
(715) 634-4440
www.freshwater-fishing.
    org

Truckee River Flyfishers
    (Reno)
*Call Reno Fly Shop for
    current contact number.*

Tahoe Truckee Fly Fishers
*Call Reno Fly Shop for
    current contact number.*

Government Resources, Nevada

Humboldt National Forest
2035 Last Chance Road
Elko, NV 89801
(775) 738-5171
www.fs.fed.us/htnf

Nevada Department of
    Wildlife (NDOW)
State Headquarters
1100 Valley Rd.
Reno, NV 89520
(775) 688-1500
www.ndow.org

NDOW Region I
380 West "B" St.
Fallon, NV 89406
(775) 423-3171
www.ndow.org

NDOW Region II
60 Youth Center Road
Elko, NV 89801
(775) 777-2300
www.ndow.org

NDOW Region III
4747 Vegas Dr.
Las Vegas, NV 89108
(702) 486-5127
www.ndow.org

U.S. Fish and
    Wildlife Service
(800) 344-9453
www.fws.gov

Nevada State Recreation Areas

Nevada Division of State
    Parks–Main Office
1300 South Curry Street
Carson City, NV 89703-
    5202
(775) 687-4384
Fax: (775) 687-4117
http://parks.nv.gov/

Cave Lake State Park
P.O. Box 151761
Ely, NV 89315
(775) 728-4460
http://parks.nv.gov/

Echo Canyon
(775) 962-5103
http://parks.nv.gov/

Floyd Lamb
(775) 486-5413
http://parks.nv.gov/

Lahontan Reservation
(775) 577-2226
http://parks.nv.gov/

Lake Tahoe
(775) 831-0494
http://parks.nv.gov/

Rye Patch Reservation
(775) 538-7321
http://parks.nv.gov/

South Fork
(775) 744-4346
http://parks.nv.gov/

Washoe Lake
(775) 687-4319
http://parks.nv.gov/

Wild Horse
(775) 758-6493
http://parks.nv.gov/

Nevada Commission
    on Tourism
401 N. Carson Street
Carson City, NV 89315
(800) 638-2328
www.travelnevada.com

Ruby Lake Wildlife Refuge
HC 60, Box 860
Ruby Valley, NV 89833
(775) 779-2237
www.fs.fed.us/htnf

Toiyabe National Forest
1200 Franklin Way
Sparks, NV 89431
(775) 331-6444
www.fs.fed.us/htnf

Government Resources, California

California Bureau of
  Land Management
2800 Cottage Way
Suite W-1834
Sacramento, CA 95825
(916) 978-4400
www.ca.blm.gov/

California Dept. of
  Boating & Waterways
2000 Evergreen
Suite 100
Sacramento, CA 95815
(916) 263-1331
http://dbw.ca.gov/

California Dept. of
  Fish & Game
1416 Ninth Street
Sacramento, CA 95814
(916) 445-0411
http://dfg.ca.gov/

California Dept. of
  Fish & Game
601 Locust Street
Redding, CA 96001
(530) 225-2300
http://dfg.ca.gov/

California Dept. of
  Parks & Recreation
P.O. Box 94296
Sacramento, CA 94296
(916) 653-6995
(800) 777-0369
www.parks.ca.gov/

California Office of Tourism
P.O. Box 1499, Dept, TIA
Sacramento, CA 95812
(800) 862-2543
http://gocalif.ca.gov/
  state/tourism/tour-
  homepage.jsp

Lake Tahoe Forest Service
35 College Drive
South Lake Tahoe,
  CA 96150
(530) 543-2600
www.fs.fed.us/r5/ltb.mu/

United States
  Forest Service
Pacific Southwest Region
1323 Club Drive
Vallejo, CA 94592
(707) 562-8737
www.fs.fed.us/r5/

References & Other Reading Material

*Terry Barron's No Nonsense
  Guide to Fly Fishing
  Pyramid Lake*
No Nonsense Fly Fishing
Guidebooks

*Nevada & Northern
  California Atlas &
  Gazetteer*
Delorme Mapping

*Fly Fishing Afoot for
  Western Bass*
Ken Hanley

Nevada Angling Guide
Richard Dickerson

Nevada Fishing Regulations

*Ken Hanley's No Nonsense
  Guide to Fly Fishing in
  Northern California*
No Nonsense Fly Fishing
Guidebooks

*Fly Fisher's Guide to
  Northern California*
Seth Norman

*California Blue Ribbon
  Trout Streams*
Amato Publications

California Fishing
Foghorn Press

California Fly Fisher
Magazine

Sierra Trout Guide
Ralph Cutter

Other Fly Fishing Resources

NDOW Radio Program
"On the Wildside of Life"

Fishing Conditions:
Ely, KDSS-FM 93
Fallon, KVLV-AM 980
Minden, KGVM-FM 99.3
Reno, KKOH AM 780
Tonopah, KHWK-FM 92.7
Winnemucca, KWNA-AM
  1400

Fly Fishing The Internet

www.amrivers.org
www.fbn-flyfish.com
www.fedflyfishers.org
www.ffa.com
www.fly-fishing-women.com
www.flyfish.com
www.flyfishamerica.com
www.flyfishing.com
www.flyshop.com
www.gofishing.com
www.gorp.away.com
www.gssafaris.com
www.ohwy.com
www.tu.org

Knots

www.earlham.edu
www.ozemail.com
www.fishnmap.com/
www.maps4u.com/news/
  2001Aug/GPSClasses.
  html

U.S. Government Resources

www.freshwater-fishing.org
www.fs.fed.us/recreation/
  map/finder.shtml
www.fs.fed.us/htnf
www.fws.gov/

Guidebooks

www.amazon.com
www.barnesandnoble.com
www.bookzone.com
www.powells.com
www.justgoodbooks.com

Air Travel

Alaska
www.alaskaair.com
(800) 426-0333

American
www.aa.com
(800) 433-7300

America West
www.americawest.com
(800) 235-9292

Continental
www.continental.com
(800) 525-0280

Delta
www.delta.com
(800) 221-1212

Northwest
www.nwa.com
(800) 225-2525

Southwest
www.southwest.com
(800) 435-9792

United
www.united.com
(800) 241-6522

USAirways
www. usair.com
(800) 428-4322

Travel Agents

www.expedia.com
www.itn.com
www.thetrip.com
www.travelweb.com
www.travelocity.com

Directories
www.fish-world.com

Where No Nonsense Guides Come From

No Nonsense guidebooks give you a quick, clear, understanding of the essential information needed to fly fish a region's most outstanding waters. The authors are highly experienced and qualified local fly fishers. Maps are tidy versions of the author's sketches.

These guides are produced by the fly fishers, their friends, and spouses of fly fishers, at No Nonsense Fly Fishing Guidebooks.

All who produce No Nonsense guides believe in providing top quality products at a reasonable price. We also believe all information should be verified. We never hesitate to go out, fly rod in hand, to verify the facts and figures that appear in the pages of these guides. The staff is committed to this research. It's dirty work, but we're glad to do it for you.

No Nonsense Fly Fishing Knots

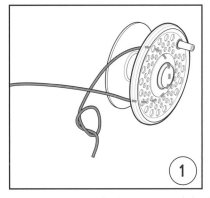 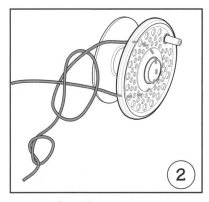 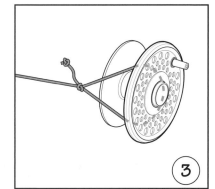

Arbor Knot: Use this knot to attach backing to your fly reel.

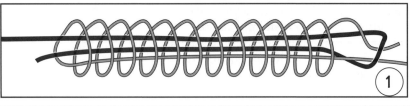

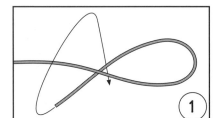

Albright Knot: Use this knot to attach backing to your fly line.

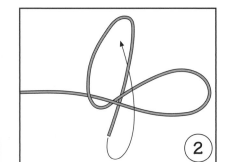

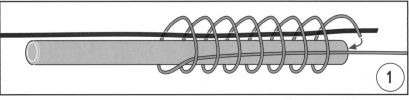

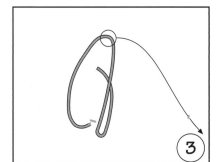

FLY LINE

LEADER

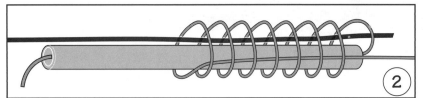

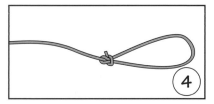

Nail Knot: Use a nail, needle or a tube to tie this knot, which connects the forward end of the fly line to the butt end of the leader. Follow this with a Perfection Loop and you've got a permanent end loop that allows easy leader changes.

Perfection Loop: Use this knot to create a loop in the butt end of the leader for loop-to-loop connections.

 70

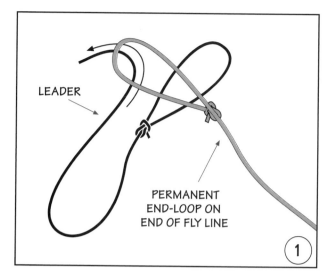

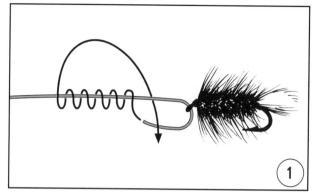

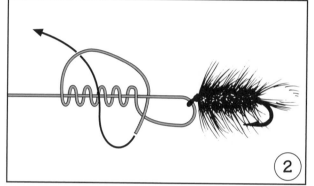

Loop-to-Loop: *Easy connection of leader to a permanent monofilament end loop added to the tip of the fly line.*

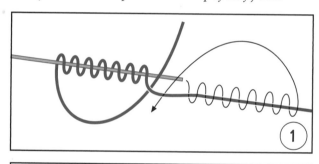

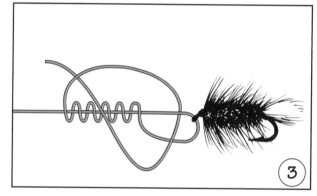

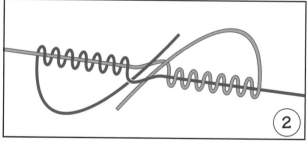

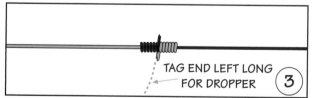

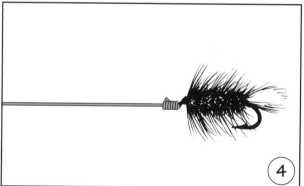

Improved Clinch Knot: *Use this knot to attach the fly to the end of the tippet. Remember to moisten the knot before pulling it up tight.*

Blood Knot: *Use this knot to connect sections of leader tippet material. Hard to tie, but worth the effort.*

Find Your Way With These No Nonsense Guides

Fly Fishing Central and Southeastern Oregon
Harry Teel

Coming Soon: The Metolius, Deschutes, McKenzie, Owyhee, John Day and 35 other waters. Mr. Teel's 60 years of fly fishing went into the first No Nonsense fly fishing guide, published in 1993 and updated, expanded and improved in 1998 by Jeff Perin. Now updated again and bigger and better than ever.

ISBN #1-892469-09-X $19.95

Fly Fishing Colorado
Jackson Streit

Your experienced guide gives you the quick, clear understanding of the essential information you'll need to fly fish Colorado's most outstanding waters. Use this book to plan your Colorado fly fishing trip, and take this guide along for ready reference. This popular title has been updated, redesigned, and is in its third printing.

ISBN #1-892469-13-8 .... $19.95

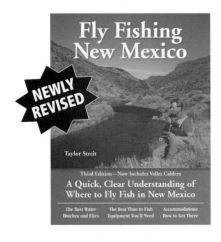

Fly Fishing New Mexico
Taylor Streit

Since 1970, Mr. Streit has been New Mexico's *foremost* fly fishing authority and professional guide. He's developed many fly patterns used throughout the region. Taylor owned the Taos Fly Shop for ten years and managed a bone fishing lodge in the Bahamas. He makes winter fly fishing pilgrimages to Argentina where he escorts fly fishers and explorers.

ISBN #1-892469-04-9 .... $18.95

Fly Fishing Utah
Steve Schmidt

Utah yields extraordinary, uncrowded and little known fishing. Steve Schmidt, outfitter and owner of Western Rivers Fly Shop in Salt Lake City has explored these waters for more than 28 years. Covers fly fishing mountain streams and lakes, tailwaters, bass waters and reservoirs.

ISBN #0-9637256-8-8 .... $19.95

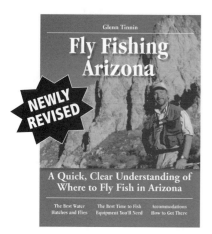

Fly Fishing Arizona
Glenn Tinnin

Arizona has a wonderful variety of waters to fly fish from the hot desert floor to cool alpine forests and higher! Here you'll find favorite trout waters from the famous Lee's Ferry to small mountain lakes. Also included are some fine reservoirs and streams where one can fly fish for bass.
ISBN #1-892469-02-2......................$18.95

Fly Fishing Southern Baja
Gary Graham

With this book you can fly to Baja, rent a car and go out on your own to find exciting saltwater fly fishing! Mexico's Baja Peninsula is now one of the premier destinations for saltwater fly anglers.
ISBN #1-892469-00-6......................$18.95

Fly Fishing California
Ken Hanley

Coming Soon: Mr. Hanley and some very talented contributors like Jeff Solis, Dave Stanley, Katie Howe and others, have fly fished nearly every top water in California. Saltwater, bass, steelhead, high mountains, they provide all you need to discover the best places to fly fish in the Golden State.
ISBN #1-892469-10-3......................$19.95

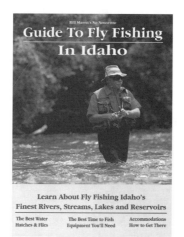

Guide to Fly Fishing Idaho
Bill Mason

The Henry's Fork, Salmon, Snake, and Silver Creek plus 24 other waters. Mr. Mason penned the first fly fishing guidebook to Idaho in 1994. It was updated in 1996 and showcases Bill's 30 plus years of Idaho fly fishing.
ISBN #0-9637256-1-0......................$14.95

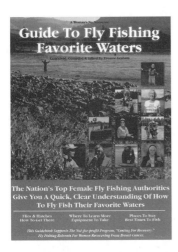

A Woman's Guide to Fly Fishing Favorite Waters

Yvonne Graham

Forty-five of the top women fly fishing experts reveal their favorite waters. From scenic spring creeks in the East, big trout waters in the Rockies to exciting Baja; all described from the female perspective. A major donation goes to Casting for Recovery, a nonprofit organization for women recovering from breast cancer.

ISBN #1-892469-03-0 ... $19.95

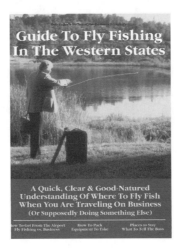

Guide to Business Traveler's Guide to Fly Fishing in the Western States

Bob Zeller

A seasoned road warrior reveals where one can fly fish within a two hour drive of every major airport in thirteen western states. Don't miss another day fishing!

ISBN #1-892469-01-4 ....$18.95

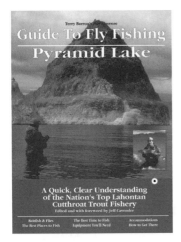

Guide to Fly Fishing Pyramid Lake Nevada

Terry Barron

The Gem of the Desert is full of huge Lahontan cutthroat trout. Terry has recorded everything you need to fly fish the most outstanding trophy cutthroat fishery in the U.S. Where else can you get tired of catching 18-25" trout?

ISBN #0-9637256-3-7 ....$15.95

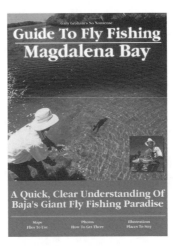

Guide to Fly Fishing Magdalena Bay

Gary Graham

Guide and excursion leader Gary Graham (Baja On The Fly) lays out the truth about fly fishing for snook in mangroves, off-shore marlin, calving whales from Alaska, beautiful birds, kayaking, even surfing. Photos, illustrations, maps, and travel information, this is "the Bible" for this unique region.

ISBN #1-892469-08-1 ....$24.95

Seasons of the Metolius

John Judy

This new book describes how a beautiful riparian environment both changes and stays the same over the years. This look at nature comes from a man who makes his living working in nature and chronicles John Judy's 30 years of study, writing and fly fishing his beloved home water, the crystal clear Metolius River in central Oregon.

ISBN #1-892469-11-1........................$20.95

Fly Fishing Lee's Ferry

Dave Foster

This colorful guide provides a clear understanding of the complex and fascinating 15 miles of river that can provide fly anglers 40-fish days. Detailed maps direct fly and spin fishing access. Learn history, boating and geology and see the area's beauty. Indispensable for the angler and intrepid visitor to the Marble Canyon.

ISBN #1-892469-07-3.....................$21.95

Dave Stanley. Photo by Robert Anderson.

Largemouth Bass

Notes

State of Nevada
Major Highway Network

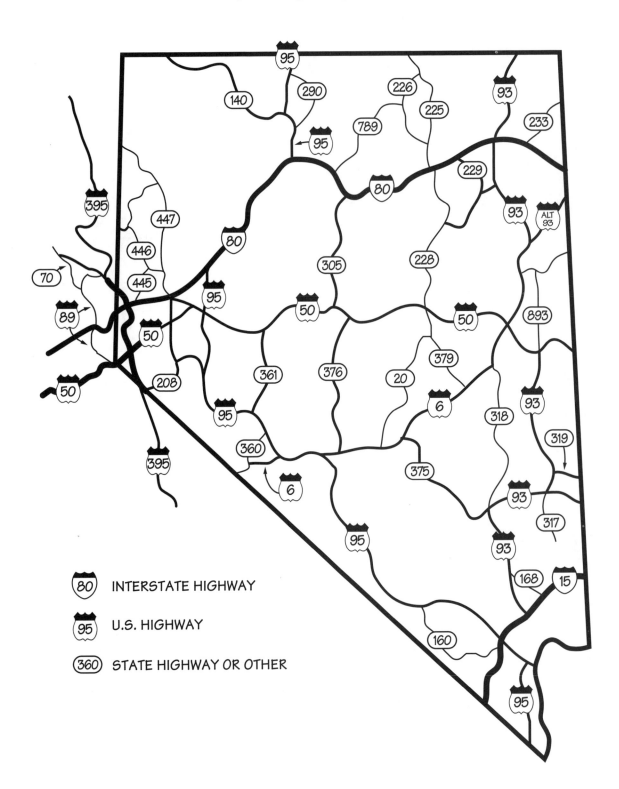

80